In *Loving Samaritans*, Terry has given the church a gift and a framework that will help move us forward as we navigate the turbulent times in which we live. Terry is honest, loving, and hopeful while facing head-on the most important issues of our day. This is an important book for this hour.

—Christine Caine, founder, Propel Women

Loving Samaritans is an incredible exploration of timeless teachings, weaving together the threads of faith, compassion, and unity. Through its poignant retelling of biblical stories, this book reignites the flame of soul-stirring conviction. It offers a powerful blueprint for embracing love as a force that transcends boundaries.

—Tim Timberlake, senior pastor, Celebration Church; author of the bestselling *The Art of Overcoming*

Although Christians are supposed to be known by our love for one another, we have somehow become known for our hate for people who don't look or vote like us, including our Christian brothers and sisters. In *Loving Samaritans*, Terry Crist calls us all back to the place where we are known by the one thing that Jesus said matters as much as how we love God: how we love our neighbor. This book is masterfully written and a must-read for all who call Jesus Lord of their lives.

—Nona Jones, author, *Killing Comparison*; preacher; tech executive

It's hard to think of a message more timely and necessary in our world today than this clarion call to radical kindness. We've all been hurt. We've all hurt others. Especially Christians. Something has to change. I particularly appreciate Terry Crist's vulnerability in the chapter "Insiders and Outsiders," his consistent focus on Jesus, and his thoughtful

commentary throughout. Here we have the brilliant mind and tender heart of a seasoned pastor grappling with one of the most important issues of our time.

—**Pete Greig,** 24-7 Prayer International

As much as you will be amazed and astonished by Terry Crist's peerless storytelling and his radical rethinking of the familiar, you will be even more amazed and astonished by the fathomless and fulsome love of Jesus. I was sad when the book ended, and will return to it like a pilgrim to a holy site, seeking ongoing inspiration and guidance.

—**Leonard Sweet,** author; professor; publisher; founder, PreachTheStory.com

In a world full of polarizing opinions and fearmongering sound bites, Pastor Terry has written a book to help the church look more like her savior, Jesus. In a world that is growing more and more polarized and tribal, we need this book. In the years that I've known Terry Crist, he has embodied the message of this book. Pastor Terry is a friend, a pastor, an orator, and so many other things. But it is undeniable that he has chosen to love Samaritans. The church needs this book. Our world needs this book.

—**Manny Arango,** pastor; speaker; author, *Brain Washed*

A national prophetic word from a national Christian pastor of a local church! With great courage, clarity, and biblical foundations, Pastor Terry Crist calls the American church and Christians to repentance and love of all neighbors. He has lived everything he is preaching; it's not just a lot of words. *Loving Samaritans* provides a path to holding on to your faith while loving those who are outside it or who live contrary to what your faith teaches. He calls us back to Jesus' life and teachings. A rare and must-read book for anyone wanting to build bridges, share Jesus, or simply love others.

—**Bob Roberts Jr.**, author; president, Glocal.net, Multifaith Neighbors Network, Institute for Global Engagement, Glocal Ventures

In *Loving Samaritans*, author Terry Crist takes readers on an emotional and inspiring journey that reaffirms our faith in Jesus' compassion, kindness, and invitation to be a good neighbor. This beautifully crafted book weaves authentic stories and personal experiences, reminding readers of the extraordinary capacity for goodness within us all. People are looking for presence over perfection. This book offers a compelling exploration of empathy, generosity, and grace. It will touch your soul, uplift your spirit, and give you hope. Terry has lived this book, and his words lovingly invite us all to do the same.

—**Jeanne Stevens,** founding lead pastor, Soul City Church

Loving Samaritans urges us to reflect on our actions and evaluate how we show love toward others. It is a thought-provoking read, evoking a sense of conviction while also providing encouragement and practical guidance. Terry courageously tackles sensitive subjects that many shy away from, bravely addressing important issues.

—**Dan Blythe,** Alpha Youth global director; author; speaker

Loving Samaritans is a clear and courageous message to awaken the body of Christ and embrace the call to love God and neighbor. Terry Crist has given us a practical perspective on how to embody Jesus' presence in our communities.

—**David Docusen,** author, *Neighborliness: Love Like Jesus. Cross Dividing Lines. Transform Your Community*

It seems as if Christians are more divided than ever. Rather than living on mission, we have become increasingly polarized from our brothers and sisters who might see social issues differently than we do. Sadly, we have created an us-versus-them culture. In his book *Loving Samaritans*, Terry Crist invites us on the journey of radical love. Using Jesus' encounter with the woman at the well and other Samaritan stories, as well as difficult circumstances from his own life, Terry offers a path for us to walk in truly living out the message of Jesus. This book is an important one!

—**Holly Wagner,** cofounding pastor, Oasis Church; founder, She Rises; author, *Find Your Brave*

Pastor Terry Crist boldly reminds the church of the radical love of Jesus and our duty to love our neighbors as ourselves.

—**Evan Craft,** Christian recording artist

My friend Terry has written a tour de force. This is not an ethereal and sanitized set of ideas disconnected from reality. What is inside is an invitation to actually deal with the world God has invited us to love. Good doctors don't ignore the pain. They go to it. In this book you are in the hands of a very good doctor. This book is a gift.

—**A. J. Swoboda** (PhD, University of Birmingham), associate professor of Bible and Theology, Bushnell University; author, *After Doubt*

loving
loving
loving
loving
loving
samaritans

terry crist

loving
loving
loving
loving
loving
samaritans

radical kindness in an
us vs. them world

■ ZONDERVAN
■ BOOKS

ZONDERVAN BOOKS

Loving Samaritans
Copyright © 2024 by Terry M. Crist

Published in Grand Rapids, Michigan, by Zondervan. Zondervan is a registered trademark of The Zondervan Corporation, L.L.C., a wholly owned subsidiary of HarperCollins Christian Publishing, Inc.

Requests for information should be addressed to customercare@harpercollins .com.

Zondervan titles may be purchased in bulk for educational, business, fundraising, or sales promotional use. For information, please email SpecialMarkets@Zondervan .com.

ISBN 978-0-310-36696-6 (softcover)
ISBN 978-0-310-36698-0 (audio)
ISBN 978-0-310-36697-3 (ebook)

Published in association with The Bindery Agency, www.TheBinderyAgency.com.

Cover design: Curt Diepenhorst
Author photo: Tony Taafe
Interior design: Denise Froehlich

Printed in the United States of America

23 24 25 26 27 LBC 5 4 3 2 1

contents

preface

Dear Church,

From my earliest memories of growing up in a pastor's home, I have loved you in all your breathtaking diversity. From storefront fellowships in urban strip malls to ancient cathedrals in historic city centers to rural parishes, I have marveled at the "smells and bells," robed choirs and worship bands, formal teaching, and contemporary preaching. There is nothing quite like the church on display before the world as the manifold wisdom of God embodied in a people. Together, despite our storied history, we have been effective in changing the world for the better.

Recently, however, we've become engulfed in diversions—partisan politics, cultural skirmishes, and fear of those who differ from us. Now is the moment to refocus. We shine brightest when serving the world, not seeking to dominate it. The words in this book are my heartfelt prophetic call back to Jesus' foundational teachings of love, compassion, and justice. As you turn these pages, may they inspire you to engage in building a church as kind and gracious as it is venerable and sacred.

With hope for our future,

Terry

Dear The Other,

If you've ever felt the cold shadow of exclusion cast by the church, this book is for you. From my earliest memories in a pastor's home, I've seen the church in all its complexity, both its beauty and its blemishes. I've witnessed communion in ancient cathedrals and community centers, heard hymns and rock anthems, seen robed priests and tattooed pastors—all reflecting the infinite facets of a God whose image we all bear.

But the church has not always been a refuge for everyone. For that, I am deeply sorry. Our history is marred by moments when we've acted less like a loving family and more like a judgmental institution. We have sometimes allowed dogma to overshadow the simple, profound message of Jesus: to love one another unconditionally.

I offer the words in this book as a step toward a new future. My hope is that as you turn these pages, you will find a renewed sense of possibility for what the church can be—a sanctuary for all, regardless of background, beliefs, or life story.

*In earnest anticipation of a more
compassionate tomorrow,*

Terry

chapter 0

high rises and elevators

missional living in a vulnerable world

The sharp ding of the elevator bell echoed in the compartment as the door slid open, revealing a young woman in a state of panic waiting to get on. She burst into the confined space, her bare feet slapping the floor. Something was wrong. Her clothes and shoes shook as she clutched them, her long hair disarrayed across her face. Mascara ran down her cheeks. Her eyes darted left and right, looking for the panel of elevator buttons.

She located the panel and frantically pressed a button, trying to shut the doors. As they slowly closed, sealing her within the protection of the elevator, a prayer of gratitude escaped her lips. "Thank you, Father. Thank you for saving my life."

As the elevator began its sluggish descent from the tenth

floor, she leaned against the wall, taking in her surroundings. That's when she noticed my wife and me standing in disbelief in the corner. Her eyes met ours, and she whispered, "He tried to kill me."

Welcome to the neighborhood.

For more than twenty years, our family had lived in the perfectly manicured cul-de-sacs of a gated community in Scottsdale, an upper-middle-class suburb about thirty minutes outside of Phoenix. All of our houses were the same. You might think you know what that means, but unless you've lived in a "master-planned community," you don't. Same architecture. Same color. Same landscaping. (If you can call red pebbles with the occasional cactus landscaping.) We placed our trash receptacles in the same place on our identical sidewalks on the same days. Tuesday for trash, Thursday for recycling.

All of this was mandated and enforced by the dreaded and omniscient homeowners association—the HOA. The HOA was the housing equivalent of the Old Testament law and was enforced religiously by the community's equivalent of the Pharisees. Oh, and did I mention that our neighborhood was exclusively white? That wasn't officially mandated by the HOA; it was the way things just were.

Our master-planned community in the suburbs was surrounded by a wall whose gate was manned by armed guards. This is a common practice in this particular city, and not because the city is dangerous. The gate was designed to insulate the neighborhood from outsiders. Yet the way our neighborhood was designed also kept us isolated from each other. It was just so easy to walk through our house, enter the garage, get in our car, drive through the gate, and leave the neighborhood without encountering a single human being. The reverse process would take you "home."

In the more affluent neighborhoods in North Scottsdale, there are even gated communities within gated communities. Judith and I once had dinner with a couple in a neighborhood within a neighborhood within a neighborhood. Three levels deep. It felt like we were in a scene from a sci-fi movie.

The suburbs served us well for many years, but then something began to feel off. Something was changing inside us, a sense that this wasn't quite the way we wanted to live. Eventually we grew weary of the mind-numbing sameness and guarded-gate isolation. We moved out of the suburbs and into a more diverse apartment building in central Phoenix.

Nothing about our new neighborhood could be considered the same. One block to the north, you find the most affluent zip code in Arizona. One block to the south, you find vulnerable neighborhoods. We live at the intersection of these distinct realities.

We bade farewell to the security and comfort of our gated suburban neighborhood, and the not-so-beloved homeowners association, for a couple of reasons. The global church we had become a part of required extensive travel, with multiple trips to Australia and Europe each year, in addition to our schedule of traveling across North America. And when I say extensive, that's coming from someone who has traveled to more than sixty countries, some as many as twenty times.

With that hectic travel schedule, we decided it would be more practical to reside in a "lock and leave" apartment in a high-rise not too far from the airport. Ironically, we made this decision just before the pandemic restricted all global travel and we ended up being grounded for a year. Now that life has returned to some sense of normalcy, we can disembark from an airplane, jump into an Uber, and be in our bedroom unpacking our suitcases in twelve minutes flat. (Yes, I've timed it, and it has become a running competition between us. I'm that guy.)

But there is another and more important reason we moved into the city.

After two decades of serving as the lead pastors of a large, multisite church, my wife and I sensed God calling us to embark on a personal mission to love and serve the city of Phoenix. Our church was already active in the city in many different ways: fostering hundreds of youths, partnering with vulnerable schools, serving refugees, operating a shelter for abused women and children, and much more. And yet despite our church's significant portfolio of social programs, something felt missing in our souls. Even though we were the directional leaders of our church's missional engagement, we felt like we were outsourcing our compassion to others— our staff, our team, our volunteers. We wanted to roll up our shirtsleeves and collaborate with God in his work within our city not by delegating the responsibility of addressing the challenges faced by our community to other members within our church but by personally coming alongside those who are in need.

As we packed our belongings to leave the familiarity of suburbia, we faced the reality that for many in our new community, living there was a matter not of choice but of economic necessity or other societal factors. This new neighborhood was our choice, but for others, it was their only option. Our relocation was more than a move; it was an immersion into a vibrant community filled with history, intricacies, and ongoing challenges. This was going to be a master class for us on relating to "the other." Understanding that our circumstances had afforded us choices that others didn't have, we reflected on how to approach our new life with sensitivity and empathy. The realization that our privilege allowed us choices fostered a deliberate, humble approach to our move. We were driven by a desire to listen, learn, and engage with our new neighbors. We were joining them in their lives, and our ambition was to be compassionate and understanding neighbors, not dogmatic religious strangers. Reading the stories of Jesus and his first followers, we're presented with a vision that transcends the comfort of gated communities and cookie-cutter neighborhoods. We see a vivid portrayal of life in all its complexity, its struggles, and its breathtaking beauty. This image stirs something profound in me, and I suspect it might in you too. It calls us toward a more fulfilling way of following Jesus, one laden with joy, surprise, and the thrilling adventure of following the Holy Spirit.

Rules of Engagement

Over the past two decades, many faith communities, with good intentions, have debated the most effective strategies to reach people. The conversation revolves around two approaches to evangelism: attractional church methods versus missional engagement. While the average churchgoer might not care much about that distinction, it influences all of us in ways we might not realize. These divergent approaches shape the way we express our faith and engage with people in our neighborhoods.

The attractional approach rides on the energy and appeal of large, dynamic church services. Supporters argue that Jesus' ability to draw significant crowds unto himself is a model to follow, suggesting that mass evangelism is the most effective way to reach the world with the gospel. This approach utilizes creativity, innovation, and marketing, merging elements from pop culture into worship services to attract nonbelievers.

On the other side, missional advocates prioritize an incarnational approach to life and ministry. Rather than adopt the strategies of a consumer society, they strive to emulate Jesus by embedding themselves within communities and living out their faith in everyday life. They desire to identify where God is at work in neighborhoods and to join him there, engaging nonbelievers within their daily routines. They believe that by engaging nonbelievers in a way that is winsome, authentic, and within the context of their day-to-day lives, people who see the gospel being embodied will come to trust in Jesus and, in turn, begin to love, serve, and influence the world in which they live.

I've weighed both sides of this debate from a place of deep conviction, and it's important to remember that sincere and godly leaders support both methods. It concerns me that we perceive these approaches as mutually exclusive when both have their value. Perhaps the greater issue is that many Christians are *neither* attractional nor missional. They haven't yet seen their place in God's unfolding story to redeem, restore, and reconcile the world.[1]

Instead of being defined by a particular ministry philosophy, shouldn't we simply strive to embody Jesus' heart in our everyday interactions?

It's clear to me that Jesus practiced a both-and approach in his ministry. He invited people to "come and see," and then he commissioned them to "go and tell." Both approaches have their place in a world that still responds to the allure of an invitation and the power of a personal testimony. Why shouldn't Christians who belong to spiritually vibrant churches pulsating with the life and energy of the Holy Spirit invite others to join them each Sunday? These churches give us an earthly picture of the heavenly party that breaks out when even just one person surrenders their life to Jesus.[2]

I also recognize that there are many people who may never receive a personal invitation to a flourishing church and, even more, that they might not be the type of person who would even respond to such an invitation. This is where the missional approach to go and tell becomes necessary. And in a post-Christian world where people are often highly skeptical, deeply cynical, and resistant to the gospel, we must engage in the even longer game of "*show* and tell." It's not enough to tell people about the radical kindness of God expressed in and through Jesus. We must demonstrate it too. Unless we demonstrate our love through actions, our words will never be perceived as genuine.

The truth is we can live missionally in the suburbs or attractionally in the city. Or we can embody both wherever we live. It's less about our location and more about embracing our mission: engaging with those around us with the love and grace of Jesus.

Even though our ministry in the suburbs bore a lot of fruit, my wife and I moved into the city longing to connect with people who were outside our previous sphere of influence. We found this opportunity in a beautifully diverse neighborhood teeming with people from every walk of life. Daily, I am reminded that the mission we've embraced is deeply communal.

Even in a big city, everyone seems to be looking for a small village.

In the hustle and bustle of a metropolis, where skyscrapers seem to burst from the soil and grow into the heavens one after another and people buzz about in ceaseless motion, there lies a universal yearning for a sense of community. This longing for a village, however, is less about geographic size and more about the feeling of belonging, the warmth of knowing your neighbors, the joy of shared celebrations, and the comfort of a support system in times of need. It's about the communal ties that bind us, the shared stories that weave the fabric of our lives, and the intimate connections that foster a sense of home and identity. It's the magic of small towns encapsulated in the vast cityscape—an island of familiarity and human connection in a sea of faces that look nothing like your own. Whether we live in the heart of a metropolis or on a quiet suburban street, our souls crave that intimate, communal connection that makes us feel grounded and a part of something larger than ourselves.

Elevator Etiquette

The neighborhood surrounding our high-rise is not the only diverse thing about our community; the building itself is filled with unique and interesting people. Our high-rise is a microcosm of humanity. Picture all of the people you cross paths with over days, weeks, and months, then envision them sharing a space. There are a lot of hopes, dreams, hurts, fears, beliefs, and behaviors packed tightly into two towers in central Phoenix. And since I ride the elevator up and down fourteen stories a few times every day, I have gotten to know most of my neighbors.

I've also realized that I have a love-hate relationship with elevators. I'm grateful not to have to walk up fourteen flights of stairs, but the button-response time drives me crazy. With almost everything else in life, you push the button once and the job is done. But with elevators, I push the button repeatedly as if I can somehow make it come more quickly. And once I get on, I don't know the proper etiquette.

If there are only two people on the elevator, do you stand on opposite sides?

If the first person is in the middle, do you retreat to a corner? Which one?

If someone is at the back, is it weird to stand directly in front of them?

Call me neurotic, but these questions plague me. And the questions don't end when the elevator doors open. What's the correct way to file out? My wife once jumped off an elevator in an LA hotel and ran straight into Mick Jagger. We were running late for a church service, she was distracted, and when the door opened, she bolted. Before I could grab her arm, she hit the legendary Mr. Jagger with her full weight. In a nanosecond, *his* life flashed before *my* eyes and I could see the inevitable headline: "Woman Pastor Maims Aging Member of the Rolling Stones." Thankfully, he was extremely gracious, she had a special moment that we will never forget, and we both learned the importance of a cautious elevator exit.

As much as I don't like elevators, at least they're better than guarded gates.

Instead of keeping people out, elevators force us closer to our neighbors.

Whether you ride the elevator in an apartment building or live in a gated community, how closely do you live to your neighbors? I'm referring not to proximity but rather to the emotional, relational, and spiritual closeness you share. I'm not asking for a survey of your property boundary, I'm asking you to survey the condition of your heart. Are you engaged with your community? Do you weep for your neighbors and rejoice with them, sharing in their sorrows and joys? Do you love them?

Some might not consider the terrified young woman who burst into our elevator as our neighbor—not technically. She didn't live in our building. During the sixty-second ride that seemed to go on forever, she shared that she had met a man at a bar and gone home with him, and something went wrong during their intimate encounter. She had fled when he went to the bathroom.

Once the elevator reached the ground floor, the young lady bolted. My wife and I ran alongside her through the lobby, around the corner, past the mail stations, and out into the guest parking garage. Frantically, she searched for her vehicle as we kept guard, fearing her assailant would arrive before she got away. After what seemed like an eternity, she found the car, and with one final sob, she climbed in and peeled out of the parking lot.

Missional Living

Living "on mission" thrusts us into the raw, sometimes brutal realities of human existence, worlds away from any storybook conclusion. This calling draws us into the difficult, often painful circumstances people endure, armed not with surefire solutions but with the courage and resolve to face uncertainty head on. Engaging people in their deepest struggles requires more than a fleeting engagement or an occasional act of kindness; it demands a profound and unwavering commitment to engage with others in their most challenging battles. Missional living is about embodying a constant and unwavering presence amid life's frailties and fractures, standing in solidarity with others in their suffering and joy. This requires us to serve as a sanctuary amid their often tumultuous and multifaceted realities, where hope and despair are intertwined. Deeply immersing ourselves in the lives of our neighbors and attentively bearing witness to their struggles and victories, we grow in our understanding of their needs. Over time, we play a role not only in easing their burdens but also in fostering transformation and healing within the communities they call home.

This missional commitment is seen in the manner in which Jesus sent his disciples into the world: like lambs amid wolves, symbolizing vulnerability yet strength. In our culture, where naked displays of power pervade everything from politics to corporate leadership—even extending into the church—the gentle fortitude of the lamb is often overlooked. Yet living as a lamb requires a strength greater than living like a wolf. Anyone can be a wolf. Anyone can dominate and devour. Anyone can prioritize their ambitions over the needs of others. Following the way of Jesus means living with a gentle, unyielding strength born of and sustained by love.[3]

At its heart, living on mission means being sent into the community to introduce the brand-new world that emanates from Jesus' life, death, and resurrection. The mission of God is his effort to rescue all of creation, reconciling it back to himself, and he invites us to join him in his work, integrating our faith into every aspect of life as a witness to the resurrection and the work of reconciliation. In this grand scheme, the church and Christians alike are responsible to faithfully embody Jesus' teachings and demonstrate their relevance to our time and place. Alan Hirsch possesses a profound understanding of the "missional-incarnational impulse" within the church, a concept he has explored in depth as the foundation for being "an authentic Jesus Movement."[4] In his seminal work, *The Forgotten Ways*, Hirsch defines the "church's true and authentic organizing principle" as "the mission of God revealed in Jesus."[5] Central to this paradigm is the belief that every church, and by extension every Christian, *exists* to serve, evangelize, and disciple the nations. We are not granted the liberty to create our own mission; we are sent to participate in God's work. God is a missionary, and he partners with the church as his emissary in the world. Christianity was a movement before it became an institution, and it thrives when moving toward hurting humanity in concert with the heart of God.

When we envision the mission of God, our minds immediately go to missionaries—people who are sent to foreign lands to share the gospel. We usually associate missionaries with crossing geographical boundaries and ministering in diverse cultural contexts. Even as we are living missionally in our own neighborhoods, it is essential for us to view ourselves as community missionaries, at least in terms of our identity. Our mission field might not be geographic but rather demographic or psychographic; it might encompass groups of people all around us in the classroom, boardroom, copy room, or fitness center who neither look nor think like we do.

Living on mission is about aligning our lives with a higher calling that extends beyond our "religious" lives and into every facet of daily existence. It's a profound movement from Sunday to Monday. It does not diminish the importance of our relationships with other believers and the value of gathering for corporate worship, communion, and biblical teaching, which, though they are not the mission, are necessary parts of our faith. Instead, the mission extends what happens in those places into the world around us. It is seeing every aspect of life—relationships, vocations, and personal resources—as potential avenues for demonstrating love, mercy, and justice.

Since moving into the high-rise, I've come to understand that living on mission can often mean navigating long, uneventful periods of routine punctuated by unexpected moments of sheer panic. Whether an interaction in the elevator is mundane or unsettling, my responsibility remains consistent: to be fully present and engaged in each fleeting moment. This may be an effortless task for some, but staying present doesn't come naturally to me.

Frequently, I find myself drifting through the day, lost in my thoughts and oblivious to those around me. I can blindly walk through a crowded shopping mall, eyes glazed over, never sharing a glance with another shopper. As I drive, miles of neighborhoods can roll by unnoticed and unappreciated. Even a simple coffee pickup becomes an automated process without a thought of asking the barista, "How is your day going?" This mode of existence is a constant reminder of the effort required to be present in our interactions and connections with others.

The Ministry of Presence

I'm not alone in my struggle to connect with others. We find ourselves in a world that's saturated with paradoxes, particularly when it comes to human connections. On the one hand, technology has ushered us into an era of ultraconnectivity, where friends, family, and even strangers from across the globe are just a click away. Social media, email, and instant messaging have woven a vast, intricate web that links us all. Yet this global web seems to have ensnared us in a state of superficiality. Our connections are often brief, fleeting, and lacking in genuine depth. We're bonded by pixels and text, a veneer that conceals our true selves. Our physical, in-person connections seem to be dwindling in this world of constant digital availability. Face-to-face conversations, heartfelt discussions, and shared experiences in the physical world are becoming rarer.

The irony of our digital age is that while we find ourselves engrossed in online conversations with people from different corners of the globe, we may be increasingly disconnected from those closest to us—our neighbors, our coworkers, and sometimes even our families. We may have hundreds of social-media friends, but we feel isolated and alone in a crowded room. The very tools that were designed to bring us closer might be driving a wedge between us, fragmenting our relationships into bite-sized, digestible interactions that are consumed and then quickly forgotten.

It is a landscape that calls for reflection and perhaps a reevaluation of what it means to be connected. Are we nurturing close relationships with the same enthusiasm we apply to online connections? Are we investing in our communities, seeking to understand and engage with those who live and work around us? These questions might lead us to a more thoughtful approach to connection, one that values depth, authenticity, and the uniquely human touch that no technology can replicate. In striving for a more balanced connection, we might rediscover the richness and warmth of human interaction that transcends the digital divide.

We've all seen that family seated around the table in a restaurant with their heads down, staring at their phones. We've all *been* that family at some point or another. We are constantly present to the demands of information, communication, technology, and entertainment, and we are increasingly absent from one another even when we exist in proximity. This phenomenon isn't new. Early researchers on this peculiarity coined the term *technoference*, everyday intrusions or interruptions by technology devices. They found that even seemingly minor distractions caused by technology were associated with lower relational satisfaction, indicating an impact on our familial bonds as we increasingly cater to the digital world's constant demands.[6]

This situation isn't restricted to our familial relationships; it affects every area of our lives. Particularly, how can we love and serve people as Jesus did if we're not fully present to them? Throughout the Gospels, we see Jesus embodying the ministry of presence, consistently making himself available to the communities he visited, even outside of his teachings and miracles. His accessibility and affability endeared him to the marginalized and powerless, including lepers, women, and children. His ministry extended beyond mere presence, but never fell short of it.

Presence, or "withness," is not just a comforting concept, it's a reality that we all have the power to share. Something spiritual happens when we connect with someone, looking past surface appearances and focusing on their humanity. It's not about grand gestures or well-crafted words, it's about authenticity, empathy, and the simple act of being there for one another.

This idea of withness transcends our daily interactions and holds significant implications for how we engage with our communities and those in need. It's not about a strategic plan or a rehearsed approach, it's about genuine connection and love. As my friend Dr. Leonard Sweet so eloquently puts it, "Withness is a way of *being* with people in all their complexities and contradictions, just as Jesus was with us. Therefore, the ultimate witness to our culture is withness."[7]

Could it be that our emphasis on witness over withness has motivated us to pressure people into conversions lacking conviction, or even to write off those who might have embraced faith given adequate time? At a time when the church is trying to discern the next great strategy to reach people, we need no better plan than just *being* with our neighbors and coworkers. The witness of the church is our withness in the community.

In a world that often feels disconnected and impersonal, the power of presence stands out as a beacon of hope and compassion. Whether it's a kid trying to make eye contact across a crowded room or a stranger opening up in an elevator, these moments of withness reflect our shared humanity and remind us what truly matters. It's not about strategies or pressures, it's about seeing, hearing, and loving one another— right here, right now.

The practice of presence is so important to me that I walked into a tattoo shop a few years ago and had the artist ink "Be here now" on my wrist as a permanent reminder. The idea was that I could glance down at any time and be reminded of the importance of being present. Even then, sometimes I fail to see it. Just as I fail to see the people I interact with daily.

A few years ago, a lengthy thread describing a moving encounter between two strangers went viral on Twitter. During one of the lowest periods in his life, Anthony Breznican found himself on an elevator with the cherished television icon Fred Rogers. Something about seeing this familiar figure made Anthony want to open up about rediscovering *Mister Rogers' Neighborhood* during a time of profound loneliness and grief.

During their short ride, Anthony summoned his courage and blurted, "Look, I just want to tell you how much you mean to me." Mr. Rogers asked, "Oh, did you grow up as one of my television neighbors?" Anthony affirmed, "Yes, I was your neighbor." With a warm smile, Mr. Rogers opened his arms wide and said, "It's great to see you again, neighbor," enveloping him in a comforting embrace. As they stepped off the elevator, Mr. Rogers paused, removed his winter scarf, and gestured toward a window seat. "Do you want to tell me what was upsetting you so?" he inquired. And there, surrounded by a lobby full of students, Anthony poured out the pain of losing his grandfather. Fred Rogers understood the power of presence.[8]

Being a good neighbor involves more than just existing near others; it requires engaging with them. Neighboring is less about physical proximity and more about presence—a meaningful way of connecting that goes beyond geographical boundaries. This connection seeks to forge genuine relationships, whether with those in your vicinity or in your digital community. Essential to this connection are active listening, understanding, and empathy, whether the people are in your high-rise or eleven time zones away. The goal is to build meaningful relationships that are genuine, heartfelt, and enduring.

In a more profound sense, this idea reflects God's relational nature, which seeks an intimate connection with his creation rather than distant observation. Being present with others means committing to recognize their inherent worth, as God does, and treating them with love, attention, and care. This presence necessitates a readiness to celebrate joys, shoulder burdens, provide comfort, and, when necessary, lovingly challenge, all while nurturing deep and lasting connections. Embracing the idea of neighboring as an act of presence focuses our attention on others as the center of our interest. As my daughter-in-law recently said, "If God had a love language, it would be *us* loving others."

In the history of the world, no one has demonstrated this behavior better than Jesus; he engaged with people in a way that made them feel as if they were the only ones in the universe. The incarnation is a testament to God's profound desire to be with us and relate with us. Because Jesus lived among us, God connects to our struggles. Jesus' experience with mockery allows him to empathize with victims of bullying. His encounter with brutality enables him to feel the pain of those suffering abuse. His voluntary embrace of poverty attunes him to the plight of the underprivileged. Through his suffering, Jesus resonates with the vulnerability of the ailing. The incarnation serves as a vivid reminder that he shares our trials, understands our challenges, and walks our path.

Although the incarnation is a cardinal doctrine, essential to the Christian faith, it is more than that. It is also an example of how we are called to be in the world. It is an example of how we should be embedded in our communities, loving and serving them, rejoicing and suffering with them.

In what might seem like an audacious claim, the Bible asserts that the church continues to embody Christ's work in the world.[9] Just as God manifested himself in Jesus, he continues to manifest himself in and through the church as we serve the world in his name.[10] This is God's plan for loving, serving, and redeeming the world: he loved the world so profoundly that he sent Jesus, who in turn commissioned his disciples to go into the world.[11] This act of sending us forth in a particular time and place signifies the ongoing incarnation of God. Thus, incarnation extends beyond God's act of bringing Jesus into our temporal and spatial realm; it encompasses his ongoing intention for each Christian's life. Dallas Willard beautifully frames it this way: "If we are going to bring Christ to our world, our cities, our neighbors, then we do it in our own person . . . where we manifest a love that is beyond human possibilities and yet is within human actuality, because God makes it so."[12]

The doctrine of the incarnation underscores the notion that the Christian faith is not an abstract theology but a lived, embodied experience. It has profound implications for our normal way of engaging in the work of spiritual renewal. There is a time and place for big, bold expressions of faith that lay claim to things like revival and ongoing reformation, but there's also a way to simply *be* in the neighborhood as God patiently works his plan and purpose. Presence, timing, and relationship are key aspects of this incarnational way of living. Our very lives are the picture of reconciliation to the people around us who are oblivious to our divine assignment.

Eugene Peterson elegantly captures this element of incarnation in his translation of John 1:14 in *The Message*: "The Word became flesh and blood and moved into the neighborhood."

Peterson's rendition accentuates the tangibility of God's love. In becoming flesh and blood and moving into our "neighborhood," God made himself relatable and accessible, closing the distance that seemed to separate the divine from the human. The incarnation transforms the perception of God from an abstract, far-off entity to a close, relatable presence, a presence that chooses to share in our joys, sorrows, trials, and triumphs.

In essence, the incarnation is God's assurance, "I am not just here *for* you, I am here *with* you." This isn't merely a theological statement, it's a deeply personal assurance. It resonates with the human heart, echoing through our shared experiences and relationships: God is not a distant observer but an intimate neighbor, fully present in our lives. The incarnation speaks to our deepest longing to be loved and to our profound fear that we might be unworthy. Through the miracle of God drawing near, we discover that we are indeed cherished and never alone.

The notion that the incarnation could shape every aspect of our personal and communal lives seems almost too vast to comprehend. When God became one of us, he demonstrated what it means to be truly human and modeled how a community should function and thrive. This example reaches into every area of our existence, guiding our individual lives and our communal experience.

It's startling to consider that God existed in a Nazarene neighborhood for three decades without being identified. This challenges our traditional approaches to mission, suggesting there's more to our calling than conspicuous proclamations of faith. Sometimes it's about silently weaving our lives into the community's fabric, living authentically, and engaging others with heartfelt connections. The mission sometimes requires bold declarations; at other times, it calls for a subtler, more relational approach. Like the one who sends us, we are playing the long game for the sake of the world.

Neighborhood Savior

We all come from places. We live in places. In first-century Israel, the land was dotted with approximately 240 closely knit communities, much like modern neighborhoods. These small villages ranged in size from just a handful of families to around one hundred residents, covering three to four acres—a scale comparable to a modern high-rise. Jesus himself resided in one such community in a place named Nahum's Village, which is known to most of us through our Bibles as

Capernaum. This was Jesus' neighborhood, the setting for his daily life. He selected the majority of his disciples from within these intimate communities, performed the majority of his miracles there, and delivered most of his sermons and parables in these settings. In every sense, Jesus was a product of his neighborhood, deeply rooted and engaged in the life of his community. He was a neighborhood kid through and through.

Though he was embedded in a neighborhood, Jesus saw a world of mission and ministry beyond it. Refusing to be confined to the block, he ventured into other communities throughout Galilee and beyond, which is how he ended up in Samaria.[13]

The Gospel of John, a beautiful, textured, and rich literary masterpiece, offers layers that cannot be fully appreciated by those of us living two millennia after it was written. This challenge invites us to engage with the story in a deeper, more personal way. While the efforts of scholars who delve into historical-critical exegesis are valuable, understanding John requires a more nuanced appreciation of its literary artistry. His distinct editorial vision emerges not only from his claim to have witnessed enough of Jesus' ministry to fill the world with endless volumes but also from his choice of stories to recount. These choices are designed to guide readers to know and believe that Jesus is the Messiah and that through faith, they may have eternal life. We must read the Gospel of John with our hearts and our heads.

In a sudden and beautiful turn of phrase, John introduces us to an unexpected movement within his writings, without any prior warning or explanation: "Now he had to go through

Samaria." But why? Why did he *have* to go anywhere? Why couldn't the Samaritans come to him as so many others did throughout the Gospels? For that matter, why do we have to take the gospel into all the world? Why can't we leave it to people far from God to find us?

Because some never will.

Samaria was unlike any other place Jesus visited. It had a painful history and an ongoing legacy of rejection and marginalization. It was the place religious Hebrew people avoided for this reason: generations earlier, invaders had taken the land, bringing in foreign peoples for resettlement and labor. This already "mixed" population intermarried with Jews, mixing their ethnicity and their religion into the bloodline of the chosen people—and all of this right in the promised land. As a result, the Jewish community hated the people of Samaria. No self-respecting Jew would have dealings with them if they could avoid it.

The Samaritans were often perceived as the other, a faceless group defined not by their individuality but by their collective identity. They were not seen as individuals with whom one could meet, befriend, or interact. Rather, they were a category, a monolithic "them," their humanity obscured by generalizations and stereotypes. Many of their Jewish neighbors would have viewed them through the lens of their different religion, appearance, and way of life.

But these distinctions were more than mere observations; they were barriers. The term *Samaritan* seemed to blot out individual characteristics, reducing a diverse community to a single, simplified label. This label was believed to tell you everything you needed to know, rendering personal engagement undesirable and even unnecessary. It was as though understanding of or empathy toward the Samaritans was out of reach or somehow inappropriate. Safer to avoid them in person, to keep them at arm's length, and perhaps even to condemn them from the comfortable distance of unfamiliarity.

Jesus, however, wasn't playing by the rules. He did not conform to the expectations or rules of the religious community of his time. He was not there to reinforce prejudices, promote discrimination, or teach the pious how to be more virtuous. Instead, his presence in Samaria was guided by a singular, compelling force: love. This love was not an abstract or generalized sentiment; it was specific, personal, and deeply passionate. God's love reaches out to real people, each with their unique stories, struggles, and complexities. The story of Jesus' encounter in Samaria doesn't merely recount a passing moment in his itinerant ministry, it illuminates a profound spiritual reality. God will not allow us to cling to our prejudices, stereotypes, or broad-brush judgments of others. Jesus' connection to the Samaritan woman breaks down barriers and puts a face to a place often reduced to a stereotype. It is a poignant reminder that God's love is not just broad, encompassing all of humanity, but also deep, reaching each individual with profound intimacy and care. It is a love that refuses to let us think of entire groups of people in abstract ways and in impersonal terms.

While we celebrate the vast embrace of God's love for the world, this story calls us to remember the depth and personal connection of that love, recognizing each person's value and significance. Sometimes our focus on the width of God's love, wide enough to surround the whole world, makes us forget about the depth of God's love for each person. There's a reason the beloved verse in John's gospel proclaiming that "God so loved the world that he gave his one and only son" is followed up with the story of that son in Samaria. God is telling us that the world is more than a sea of humanity.[14] And just as Jesus saw this woman, with all of her pain, complexity, and humanity, we are called to see the faces around us.

What if we saw the world not merely as a faceless mass of people but as a tapestry of individual faces, each cherished by God? How might such a perspective transform our understanding of community, influence national conversations, and shape global awareness? What positive impact might it have on the quality and authenticity of our daily interactions? By recognizing the sacred worth of each person, we can enrich our souls and create a world more aligned with the love that pursues us all. This book is more than a call to mere empathy, it is an invitation to radical love, mirroring Jesus' love affair with the Samaritans. It's about recognizing the special nature of every person we encounter, regardless of their appearance or behavior. It's about seeing others as God sees them and loving them as he loves them, fully and unconditionally. This is the profound message of the gospel: the story of a God who loves not in the abstract but in the real, the raw, the messiness of our world without reservation or retreat.

Why does this matter?

Because the world has a face. And in this story, it is the face of a woman at a well, waiting to be seen, heard, and loved.

chapter 1

unlikely companions

moving toward the other

*Now Jesus learned that the Pharisees had
heard that he was gaining and baptizing more
disciples than John—although in fact it was
not Jesus who baptized, but his disciples. So
he left Judea and went back once more to
Galilee.*

—John 4:1–3

The young lady reached across the table and pointed
her finger inches from her classmate's nose. Jabbing the
air to accentuate the acrimony behind each word, she spat
out the dreaded phrase, "You hypocrite!" Her opponent was

undeterred. Placing both hands on the table, he leaned forward for emphasis as he snarled back, "You have no right to judge me, you pharisee!"

Most of us watching this heated exchange were a little confused. Weren't they accusing each other of the same thing? As far as we knew, the Pharisees were the original hypocrites. This felt like a matchup between two kids hurling "I know you are, but what am I?" at each other, but with carefully chosen Bible verses as javelins. I waited for someone to land the final blow with "It takes one to know one!" We were one step away from someone being beseeched.

Long before I went to seminary, I attended one of the small colleges within our denomination. I was allowed to test out of most classes, and I planned to spend only one year enrolled. I settled in quickly and began attending third-year classes with all the enthusiasm of a young dreamer on the fast track to changing the world.

That lasted about six weeks.

It wasn't long before tribes formed, lines were drawn, insiders were identified, and outsiders were labeled.

In places where we seek enlightenment, we often stumble into a culture of judgment.

Unbeknownst to me then, Bible colleges are often fertile breeding grounds for Pharisaism. Despite my experience teaching and even presiding at these institutions, I've never seen a deliberate intent to raise pharisees. Still, as Rich Stearns, former president of World Vision, insightfully puts it, "Every generation of Christians recreates the Pharisees.... Judging is so much easier than genuine empathy and compassion."[1]

Bible colleges, by nature, aim to instill specific interpretations of Scripture and ministry practices. This can lead to a rigid indoctrination, which often reflects the denomination or religious movement they were established to preserve. This is not unlike the Pharisees in the first century.

Later, when I went to seminary, I realized that graduate schools lean the other way. Often they "dis-indoctrinate" students through higher biblical criticism and an unhealthy cynicism of the church. The whiplash of being indoctrinated in college only to have those very conclusions challenged in graduate school made me realize that we desperately need a new model of biblical education that balances orthodoxy and orthopraxy. Perhaps then students will emerge from their educational experience with a richer, deeper, more well-rounded faith and a commitment to the global church, not just their local church or denomination.

Let me proudly confess—I am a Bible nerd. My heart beats faster as I read the riveting narratives of Scripture. After years—indeed, a lifetime—of immersing myself in these holy words, I am still spellbound by the idea that the God of the universe chose to reveal himself to us on something as ordinary as paper. It's as if he whispered his divine secrets through ink on costly, bloodstained parchment, sharing his heart in the stark contrast of black and red. Every sentence, every word resonates with his grand plan—illuminating the nature of our existence, exposing our fallibility, and reaffirming his loving desire to redeem us and renew this beautiful planet. The Bible's profundity is unparalleled; not a sentence exists without intent. Each word holds a revelation, especially when understood within the context it was written.

Who Are These People?

Have you ever found yourself caught up in heated debates or conflicts labeling others as hypocrites or pharisees? What if there's more to the story than meets the eye? Let's explore how understanding the dynamics between the Pharisees and Samaritans can help us navigate the complexities of our own relationships and communities.

In the opening chapters of John's gospel, Jesus encountered two people at the opposite ends of the spectrum: the Pharisees and the Samaritans. Despite their differences, these groups, like many polarized factions today, were not as far apart as they seemed. In John 3, a Pharisee named Nicodemus went out of his way by night to ask Jesus some questions that were probing his heart. In the following chapter, Jesus went out of his way to listen to a Samaritan woman ask probing questions of her own. Nicodemus and the Samaritan woman could not have been more different. He was a wealthy, respected, educated Jewish religious leader, and she was a vulnerable, marginalized Samaritan woman with a complicated sexual history. Yet Jesus had a deeply personal conversation with each of them.

The juxtaposition of these stories emphasizes the contrast between the two characters and their communities. Jesus willingly engaged in meaningful conversations with both individuals, demonstrating his readiness to interact with people unlike him, even those who might be considered at the extremes in a society, much like those on the Far Left or the Far Right today. This challenge confronts us in our own lives, doesn't it?

When was the last time you ventured beyond your trusted circles and engaged in deep, meaningful conversations with people who hold different views? Can you recall an instance when you spoke with a MAGA supporter, an antifa member, a Christian nationalist, or an atheist? Perhaps even a Pilates instructor or a CrossFit member? *Okay, maybe those last ones were a bit too much.*

The richness of our conversations lies not in the similarities we share but in the differences we encounter. Jesus constructed a bridge between these polarities, teaching us a strategy to navigate our current state of polarization. His profound theological discussions with a Pharisee and a Samaritan highlight the potential to bridge apparent contradictions and find common ground.

Grace is most at home in the space between extremes.

Furthermore, the interactions between Jesus, Nicodemus, and the Samaritan woman underscore the significance of humility and openness. Jesus approached both individuals with a genuine desire to understand and learn, revealing that these qualities are crucial for fostering meaningful exchanges. Humility is always the basis for meaningful conversations. Both of these conversations were held in the highest regard on the basis of profound humility, and they opened the door to a deepened understanding of his message.

The lessons we learn from these interactions apply to how we engage diverse perspectives in our own relational contexts. Our daily encounters with different points of view can be difficult to navigate, but by following Jesus' example, we can turn these moments into catalysts for growth in wisdom and understanding. Instead of seeing differences as obstacles, we can see them as possibilities. This move from a focus on differences to an acceptance of commonalities not only deepens our capacity for empathy and insight but also opens up the possibility of genuine community and meaningful connections.

The Pharisees and Samaritans had more in common than they might have been willing to admit. Both groups were descendants of Jacob and adhered to a monotheistic religion, worshiping Yahweh, the God of Israel. They each held the Torah, the first five books of the Hebrew Bible, as sacred, although their acceptance of other religious texts diverged. Both Pharisees and Samaritans anticipated the coming of the Messiah, even as their understanding of his mission varied. They both valued temple worship but disagreed on the rightful location—Jerusalem for Pharisees and Mount Gerizim for Samaritans. And both groups strove to maintain their unique identities and religious practices amid changing times.

Jesus was relationally vested in both the Pharisees and Samaritans because they were equally in need of his love and grace. Yet each group labeled him as a member of the opposite one.[2] He was often viewed as aligning with those considered "other." Today, in contrast, the trend is to claim Jesus as a member of one's own group, to co-opt him as the poster boy for our own ideologies.

Throughout his ministry, Jesus consistently demonstrated a fearless willingness to connect with "the other"—the outcasts, the marginalized, the overlooked. Where society built barriers, he built bridges. Whether dining with tax collectors, conversing with Samaritan women, or healing lepers shunned from society, he sought out the most misunderstood or rejected people. His actions challenged societal norms and exemplified the principle of inclusive love and acceptance. This fearlessness in embracing the other was grounded in his profound understanding that everyone, irrespective of their societal status, carries an inherent worth and therefore is worthy of respect.

If fear of associating with the other is entrenched within *us*, it's necessary to investigate its roots. Is this fear a result of ingrained societal norms, or does it stem from a lack of familiarity with those we view as distinct? Could it be a manifestation of a fear of being judged and rejected ourselves if we align with those deemed outside the norm? A thoughtful examination and honest evaluation of these fears is essential. Doing so, we not only gain insight into our inner reservations but also take significant strides toward overcoming them, enabling us to love, serve, and minister to others without hesitation.

The Pharisees and Samaritans represent people on opposite sides of a cultural divide, firmly committed to their worldviews and quick to hurl insults at whoever disagrees. Some may think we live in times of unprecedented tension where our faith is under attack more than ever, but the Pharisees and Samaritans would beg to differ. Their stories fit in perfectly with what we all encounter every day.

The Samaritans

The history of the Samaritans dates back to the time of the kings. After the peaceful reign of King Solomon, his son Rehoboam took the throne, marking a decline in the kingdom.

In the tenth century BC, the kingdom was divided into Israel in the north and Judah in the south, each with its own ruler.

Despite repeated warnings from prophets, both kingdoms became corrupt and sinful. In the eighth century BC, the Northern Kingdom was conquered by the Assyrians and its people were taken into captivity in the city of Halah.[3] To expand his empire, the king of Assyria brought people from other nations, such as Babylon, Kuthah, Avva, Hamath, and Sepharvaim, to intermarry with the Jews who remained in the north. These new inhabitants worshiped both Yahweh and the gods of their native lands, blending their religions with the Jewish faith.

The original name of the Northern Kingdom was Israel, and its capital city was first Shechem, then Penuel, and finally Tirzah. But when Omri became king, he built Samaria as the new capital city, which remained the capital until its fall to the Assyrians.[4] Over time, the people of the Northern Kingdom came to be known as the Samaritans because of the name of their capital.[5]

About 130 years after the Northern Kingdom fell to the Assyrians, the Southern Kingdom, Judah, whose inhabitants were called the Jews, fell to the Babylonians. They were taken into exile. After 70 years, the Persians conquered the Babylonians, and the Persian king Cyrus allowed some Jews to return to Judah to rebuild the temple in Jerusalem.[6] When they started rebuilding, the interethnic Samaritans offered to help because they had been sacrificing to the Lord as well, but the Jews refused to let them participate in the project.[7] In retaliation, the Samaritans bribed officials to sabotage the Jews' plans and even sent a letter to the king of Persia asking him to stop their rebuilding efforts.[8]

Later, when Nehemiah returned to Jerusalem to rebuild the walls, the Samaritans taunted him and fought against the rebuilding efforts. This was the start of long-lasting animosity between the Jews and the Samaritans. Isn't it amazing that centuries later we're still fighting over walls and refusing to work with the "others" in our lives?

The Pharisees

The Pharisees emerged during a time of revival in Jewish life after the Babylonian exile. This revival was marked by a greater concern for the law and the emergence of two main religious groups. The Zaddikim, also known as the righteous ones, followed only the written law of Moses (the Torah), while the Chasidim, or pious ones, believed in both the written and oral laws of the prophets and rabbis. The Zaddikim eventually split into the Sadducees and Karaites, while the Chasidim became the Pharisees and Essenes.

The term "Pharisee" originated during the time of John Hyrcanus, who briefly identified himself with a small group of zealous men on the Sanhedrin known as the Perushim, or separated ones. The Pharisees were religious separatists who avoided contamination by separating themselves from unclean places, people, and ideas. And they required others to do the same. They served as custodians of Israel's culture and guardians of Moses's law, preserving the country's identity and filling in the gaps in the written law for the practical needs of life.

Being the people of the one true God during a time of foreign rule was a complex challenge for the Jews. The downfall of their nation and the lack of clarity in the written law regarding new social, religious, and ethical questions raised concerns about the reliability of God's faithfulness and promises. The Pharisees saw separation as the only way to remain faithful and maintain the ancient ways of Judaism. They separated themselves from the rest of the culture to protect their identity and experience God's blessings once again.

The questions the first-century Jews struggled with seem all too familiar to those of us who have watched the end of an era, the departure of the "nones," and the zealous attempts of civil religionists to "take America back for God" as a response to our need for a genuine revival. We are in uncharted waters in our nation. Our spiritual decline has not only affected our public institutions, but it has also impaired our personal witness as Christians. Perhaps we can understand why the Jews looked to the Pharisees for spiritual guidance during a time of social upheaval. When faced with spiritual decline, we are tempted to turn inward to protect ourselves instead of loving, serving, and reaching out to the people we feel are corrupting society.

By the time John wrote his gospel, the Pharisees were a large and influential religious-political party in Israel. According to the historian Flavius Josephus, there were about six thousand people in their group, which made their influence no small thing in Israel. Originally, they were just a group of religious students who wanted to preserve God's ways among God's people.

Just like the zealous students at my small denominational Bible college.

I think there's something noble about the desire to preserve God's ways even though it often leads to unintended consequences. I think we all can appreciate the efforts of people who seek to preserve the best of what we love and value. Imagine someone in your family assuming responsibility for its future survival. Picture them saying, "I'm grateful for our family. Even though our parents aren't perfect, they've done a wonderful job of loving and leading us. I've been taught right from wrong. I find meaning in our traditions. And I want to take the responsibility to ensure that future generations continue this legacy. So I will teach our values, impart our wisdom, and preserve our family culture. And I will monitor all behavior to ensure that nothing is lost in the next generation."

When we look at it that way, it doesn't sound *so* bad, does it?

Who doesn't want to preserve the best of their family traditions? The Pharisees, to their credit, shared this desire, not for their own families or legacies but for the people of God. They were driven by a passion to "take back their nation" for God, yearning for a revival of right living and a unified pursuit of holiness. While their intentions were noble, it is crucial to learn from their mistakes in order to avoid repeating them. As Larry Osborne, the founder of North Coast Church, cautions, "If we fail to understand how spiritually impressive the Pharisees were, we will remain blind to the danger of becoming like them. We'll assume that their tragic transformation from passionate defenders of God into mortal enemies could never happen to us."[9]

Pharisaism is characterized by legalism, a strict adherence to rigid doctrine and religious rituals, and it comes at the expense of human well-being. It polices the actions of others to ensure adherence to God's standards, leading to the judgment and rejection of those who fall short. While legalism may seem impressive and well intentioned, its true nature is often unnoticed until it inflicts harm.

Legalism is a form of spiritual carbon monoxide: it poisons the atmosphere by choking out love.

Pastor and theologian Timothy Keller warns about the persistence of Pharisaism in contemporary evangelical churches, stating, "We tend to draw conservative, buttoned-down, moralistic people. The licentious and liberated or the broken and marginal avoid church. That can mean only one thing. If the preaching of our ministers and the practice of our parishioners do not have the same effect on people that Jesus had, then we must not be declaring the same message that Jesus did."[10]

This indictment makes me wonder: Are our churches attracting the "conservative, buttoned-down, and moralistic" because we resemble the Pharisees more than Jesus? Within the gospel accounts, Jesus reserved his most scathing condemnations for religious leaders who focused solely on external conduct, failing to examine their own hearts or address the oppressive systems they imposed upon others.

True Holiness

Despite the religious clout the Pharisees had in first-century Israel, when the word *pharisee* is hurled as an insult in a Bible college cafeteria, it's pretty clear that the modern world doesn't think too highly of this historical group. In our culture, a pharisee has come to represent anyone who is self-righteous, legalistic, judgmental, and hypocritical. Not only is this term weaponized in religious circles, but it's also used with deadly precision in the political arena.

The 2020 presidential election was marked by a particularly contentious showdown between Democratic candidate Pete Buttigieg, an Episcopalian, and Republican candidate Mike Pence, an evangelical Christian. Buttigieg publicly branded Pence as a pharisee, drawing on a term laden with biblical significance, and went further to accuse the entire Republican party of hypocrisy, alleging a failure to practice what they preach. For both candidates, who openly identify as Christians, these were not mere political jabs but serious moral accusations. The exchange highlighted the deep divisions not only in political ideology but also in the understanding and application of faith principles. It served as a reminder of the complex interplay between politics and faith, and how differing interpretations of Christian values can lead to starkly contrasting worldviews.

In a subsequent interview with the *Washington Post*, Buttigieg said, referring to the New Testament, "There's an awful lot about the Pharisees in there. . . . And when you see someone, especially somebody who has such a dogmatic take on faith that they bring it into public life, being willing to attach themselves to this administration to gain power, it is alarmingly resonant with some New Testament themes, and not in a good way."[11]

This is not intended to affirm Buttigieg's description of Mike Pence. (I've met the former vice president on a couple of occasions, and he seems like a kind and compassionate leader with a well-grounded faith.) And to be perfectly honest, there's a little pharisee in all of us, at least according to Buttigieg's description. For some of us, present company included, there's a lot of Pharisaism lurking in the shadows of our faith. We all bring our deeply held beliefs into whatever we do in life, ministry, relationships, and vocation. As well we should. The issue is not how dogmatic our convictions are but how we seek to impose those beliefs on others.

Can we hold our own deep-seated convictions while maintaining a gracious and kind spirit toward people who disagree?

Can we embody grace and truth in a world that demands allegiance to one or the other?

Can we resist grasping for the power of the insider and move with love toward the outsider?

According to the Pharisees, holiness was defined by what we abstain from, what we are against. But Jesus saw holiness as what we are for, what we give ourselves to—specifically, love, justice, mercy, and hospitality. This conflicting definition of holiness brought Jesus and the Pharisees into heated debates. It's an argument that continues across dining tables, in coffee shops, and on college campuses today. Many of us think that holiness is about what we do or don't do, our own personal behavior code. And yet Jesus teaches that the holiest people are the ones who love others well.

Demonstrating holiness means lovingly extending a helping hand to people in need rather than isolating oneself from others to avoid moral contamination.

Throughout the Gospels, Jesus puts the full responsibility on the insiders within the religious community to move toward the irreligious outsiders with love, grace, and truth, and not the other way around. In the stories of the lost sheep, the lost coin, and the prodigal son, Jesus shows us a picture of our responsibility as insiders to seek out the lost, the wayward, the outsider.[12]

Caring little about their comfort, Jesus sent his followers into the world like helpless sheep among evil wolves. And he didn't instruct them to weaponize their faith through persuasive arguments, polemics, or political power to overcome the evil in the world. Instead, he instructed them to befriend people, enter their homes, and extend peace to their households.

When you think about it, the Pharisees had a lot in common with Jesus. They both promoted a practical faith. They both valued righteousness. They both sought to honor God. Over time, however, the Pharisees became self-righteous and judgmental—nothing at all like Jesus. They moved from preserving God's ways in their own lives to legislating God's ways in everyone else's lives. They fashioned themselves into a spiritual tribunal that decided who God should accept and who he shouldn't.[13]

Yet despite their failings, the Pharisees weren't *all* wrong.

Yes, I said it.

The Pharisees weren't *all* wrong.

The problem is that we have gotten them all wrong. We often unconsciously caricature groups we don't fully understand or agree with, creating exaggerated representations of who they truly are. This is what has been done to the Pharisees and to countless other groups throughout history. This pattern often arises from a reluctance to undertake the challenging but necessary work of initiating conversations with people whose views differ from ours.

Acknowledging this tendency, we can see that the answer lies in a genuine understanding of people who think, live, and believe differently than we do. It's not enough to merely know *about* these individuals; we must endeavor to truly know them. This involves engaging in sincere conversations and listening to their perspectives, cultivating a nuanced understanding that dispels reductive stereotypes. When we get to know people, we learn to see past our differences and labels and to appreciate who they are as complex, multifaceted human beings. This not only prevents dismissiveness toward their ideas, beliefs, and values but also paves the way for meaningful dialogue and mutual respect and empathy.

The Pharisees, in their encounters with the Samaritans, were consumed by a profound disdain for those who contradicted their beliefs. In our own lives, we might find certain groups that evoke similar feelings of outrage. Who are they? Who forms the "them" in your "us versus them" narrative? Who do you find yourself resenting? Who do you perceive as a threat to your values or lifestyle? Their presence on your news feed or TV screen might incite a visceral reaction, fueled by fear of the potential changes they could bring to your nation, your culture, or even your family.

Imagine if you could witness Jesus attending the next gathering of that very group. Instead of approaching them with condemnation or a desire to shut them down, he goes with the intention to engage in conversation and build personal relationships. He seeks to understand their perspectives, gently challenges their assumptions, and extends love and grace. What would it look like if we followed his example? What if we sought to engage people we perceive as different or even adversarial? How might our willingness to listen, learn, and build bridges transform our interactions and ultimately contribute to a more compassionate and just society? The power of conversation and connection has the potential to transcend divisions and foster a deeper understanding of one another as fellow human beings on this journey of life.

When we choose to love people who are different from us, we are loving not just them but also Jesus himself.

Boundaries and Biases

Two key encounters occurred between Jesus and the Pharisees just before his journey through Samaria. One was an encounter with a specific Pharisee, and the other was more of the Pharisees' reaction to what Jesus was doing. They would have been appalled if Jesus had told them that his next meeting was with a Samaritan woman at a well. These stories of Jesus with the Pharisees help us to understand a little bit better Jesus' state of mind when he went to Samaria. *Yes, I hear the absurdity in that—as if anyone could understand his state of mind.*

The first event was an encounter with a prominent member of the Pharisees.[14] We have come to know him as Nicodemus, a prominent, highly educated, presumably wealthy leader in the Jewish community.[15] This would have distinguished Nicodemus from most of the other Pharisees, who were primarily blue-collar workers with a few middle-class businessmen in the mix. Nicodemus's wealth and status would have allowed him the freedom to approach Jesus anytime during the day, yet nighttime was his chosen moment.

Nicodemus was unlike the stereotypical Pharisee we see attacking Jesus in the Gospels. He was a cautious, curious seeker, while they were hostile to Jesus' message and

threatened by his popularity. Concerned about the consequence of being seen with Jesus, Nicodemus approached him
at night. Daytime conversations between the Pharisees and
Jesus were often combative, and Nicodemus appeared eager
to engage him in a meaningful discussion. The time of day
Nicodemus chose to approach Jesus also has a deeper meaning. Night is symbolically associated with spiritual darkness
in the Gospel of John.

Nicodemus risked his comfort, his safety, his power, and
his prestige on this quest to find the Teacher. And when he
spoke with Jesus, he didn't dig down farther into his talking
points or toe the party line; instead, he approached Jesus with
curiosity and openness. He asked questions and was brave
enough to listen to the answers. Nicodemus was an insider
who found Jesus among the outsiders.

The second event is less defined than Jesus' encounter with Nicodemus—it almost seems inconsequential in
comparison—and yet it provides insight into the tension Jesus
was facing.

At this point, Jesus' ministry was growing, and people were
coming to him in droves. Following his time in Jerusalem,
he led his disciples to the Judean countryside for a baptismal service. While there, he found out that the Pharisees felt
threatened by Jesus' growing popularity. They were upset
by how many more baptisms he performed than John the
Baptist.

The more things change, the more they stay the same.

It's been two thousand years since this moment, and religious sects are still arguing over head counts and baptismal
records. And it has driven some sincere and gifted people

right out of ministry, just as it drove Jesus out of the Judean countryside. Even more, the harsh judgmental tone of many in the evangelical community toward certain sinful behaviors has driven many younger millennials out of the church and into the world. When are we going to find a better way?

From these exchanges between Jesus and the Pharisees, and his individual encounters with Nicodemus and the Samaritan woman, we begin to understand the path Jesus was embarking upon—a journey that would challenge boundaries and confront biases. This story offers us more than a record of his movements through John's gospel; it presents to us a lens through which we can examine our own divisions, prejudices, and biases. As we trace Jesus' steps from Jerusalem to Samaria, a question arises: What would it mean to follow in his footsteps, to see beyond "us" and "them," and to embrace every person on our journey with love and understanding?

The contours of that transformative journey start with us, not them.

The journey from *your* Judea to *your* Samaria may be the most important one you ever make. It carries with it immense potential for transformation—for you, and for everyone you encounter along the way. Imagine a world where we prioritize understanding over judgment, where we seek common ground instead of emphasizing differences. How would our interactions, relationships, and communities be transformed if we chose to engage one another with empathy, respect, and a genuine desire to learn? As we continue on this journey, I want you to consider how embracing conversation over caricature can bridge divides and bring us closer to the practice of Jesus.

chapter 2

insiders and outsiders

seeing self, serving others: a world of difference

Now he had to go through Samaria.
—John 4:4

My kindergarten photo is a 1970s classic. I sport a pageboy haircut that looks like my mom used a bowl when she cut it, a floppy collared shirt with a white undershirt showing, and a goofy expression that looks like I've been taken hostage by the educational system. And then there's something else, which wasn't a byproduct of the era: I had a face full of freckles. *Where did all of these freckles come from?* I was the only one in the family with freckles. My dad looked like a handsome young Elvis (not to be confused with the other iterations of Elvis), my mom had a beautiful olive complexion, and my younger brother was a cute blond kid. And then there was me.

Under the best of circumstances, school pictures rank right up there with driver's license and passport photos, but mine seemed especially bad—even to a kindergartener.

First grade was going to be tough.

Despite being born into a loving home, I never felt like I belonged. I often wondered if I had been adopted, which deeply troubled my parents, who went to great lengths to assure me I was, in fact, their biological child. For some reason, their reassurance didn't satisfy me. I just didn't fit in, anywhere. And this wasn't something I felt only at home; it extended into every other aspect of my young life. Regardless of how many friends I had or how popular I was among my peers, this feeling persisted well beyond my adolescence.

As I progressed into my teenage years, I often wondered, "Why don't I belong anywhere? Why do I always feel like an outsider?"

I've been told this is a common feeling that almost everyone experiences at least once in life. Some people experience it because they are extremely introverted. (Check.) Others experience it because they are highly empathic and sensitive to the moods of others. (Check.) Others experience it because they are nonconformists. (Check. Check.) And still others experience it because they are disconnected from themselves, not others. (Hmm.) Social scientists hypothesize that most children begin to conceive of themselves as separate entities with unique identities around age four or five. This higher level of thinking is displayed when they start to recognize themselves in a mirror sometime around age two.

They are becoming aware of their appearance and learning that this is how others see them. Self-consciousness takes root when they realize the fundamental discrepancy between how they feel on the inside and how they're viewed by others. It's not a coincidence that this is also around the same time that children start hiding their faces in photographs and acting anxious around strangers. There seems to be an innate connection between being seen and wanting to hide.

From our earliest days, our sense of self is shaped by those around us. Family, friends, and society all contribute to our understanding of who we are. This process of self-discovery is intricately linked to the concept of mirroring, as eloquently described by nineteenth-century French poet Arthur Rimbaud. He famously proclaimed, "I is another," suggesting that our self-awareness develops through seeing ourselves reflected in the eyes of others. Our identity becomes intertwined with their perceptions and reactions.

Yet as we journey through life, a curious phenomenon occurs. The mirroring that helped us form our sense of self gradually gives way to a growing self-awareness that turns our focus inward. We become absorbed by our own thoughts, emotions, and desires, which can lead to a diminished ability to see ourselves through the eyes of others. Our perspective becomes distorted, and our understanding of both ourselves and others becomes skewed.

This shift in self-perception holds profound consequences for our interactions with others. When we view ourselves solely through our own lens, we risk losing empathy and failing to recognize the rich inner worlds of those around us. Our interactions can become transactional, driven solely by self-interest and personal gain. We might objectify others unwittingly, reducing them to tools or obstacles in our pursuit of success or pleasure. This detachment from their perspectives perpetuates our sense of isolation and contributes to a broader pattern of societal dehumanization.

This objectification of others extends beyond snap judgments based on appearances. It infiltrates our daily lives through the commodification of individuals, reducing them to objects for our consumption or pleasure. Whether it's how we treat service-industry workers, celebrities, church staff members, or people in subordinate positions, their worth is often determined by their usefulness in fulfilling our desires or meeting our needs. This objectification perpetuates a harmful power dynamic, reinforcing in us the idea that some individuals exist purely as instruments for our satisfaction, causing us to disregard their autonomy, emotions, and humanity.

Objectification is dehumanizing, and if you've ever experienced it, perhaps you still carry the scars.

We dehumanize others through social media and online discourse, workplace dynamics, stereotypes and prejudices, and mundane interactions in which we interrupt each other, disregard opinions, ignore boundaries, or overlook the emotional states of the people around us.

Seeing people as objects useful only in relationship to our lives makes it easy to justify judging, demeaning, labeling, or even seeking to "cancel" their existence, all behaviors that further their outsider status. We live in the age of social dehumanization, and social media has made this easier to accomplish now than at any other point in history. Some shred of common decency may hold us back from openly mocking someone to their face, but that courtesy doesn't apply to how we interact online. We deceive ourselves into forgetting that there is a real person with real feelings and vulnerabilities on the other side of the screen.

Online interactions have transformed the way we relate to people, according to Tal Orian Harel, Jessica Katz Jameson, and Ifat Moaz of the Hebrew University.[1] They studied the impact of social media on our perceptions and found that online platforms contribute to the dehumanization of individuals and groups. This dehumanization is seen in the three stages of Terrell Northrup's "identity in intractable conflict" theory.

The first stage, known as "threat," is when one group perceives the other as a threat to their identity. In the second stage, "distortion," the message from the other group is distorted and not given an honest evaluation. Finally, in the third stage, "rigidification," people become entrenched in their beliefs and view the other's ideas as unworthy of respect, leading to dehumanization and a desire to cancel or remove the other person from the conversation.

According to Harel, Katz, and Moaz, the dehumanization of one another through online interactions is a daily occurrence. Our social media profiles are nothing more than a collection of pixels, a screen name, a follower count, and a likes count, lacking the emotions and humanity that we possess in real life. Our online presence reduces us to mere demographics, making it easy for us to be dehumanized by others and, in turn, to dehumanize others.

I've kept a fairly low profile on social media as an attempt to avoid the divisiveness, which is so prevalent on the medium, but that hasn't kept the mob from coming after me.

One Sunday a couple of years ago, when one of our staff pastors was leaving our church, I was earnestly praying over their family during worship. Some might suggest I was a bit dramatic in my attempt to acknowledge the gravity of the moment. Someone who didn't have the best interests of our church at heart took a clip from the online service, ripped it out of context, turned it into a meme, and shared it with tens of thousands of others in an attempt to publicly ridicule me.

It worked.

The online trolls came out in full force, and the humiliation was painfully effective. Suddenly, I felt like an outsider all over again. It was shocking to see the judgment leveled from people who assumed the worst without taking time to learn the context. What stunned me the most was the source: it was another minister who decided to position me as an outsider. And my painful encounter with Christian cancel culture was minimal compared with what some others have experienced.

How we view other people really matters. If we view others as fundamentally and essentially different from us, it becomes effortless to treat them with disdain. We regard them as background figures in the narrative of our own lives, dispensable extras. But when we grasp that every person we encounter is not unlike us—carrying the same hopes, fears, dreams, desires, longings, and anxieties—any trace of superiority or self-centeredness fades away. In this realization, the distinction between insiders and outsiders dissolves.

The truth is that I'm not the main character in the story of the universe—Jesus is. The rest of us are all participants in a shared narrative and equally significant characters. Recognizing this truth alleviates the pressure we often place on ourselves. It also transforms how we engage another person, whether it's the Starbucks barista or someone behind a social-media avatar.

Jesus views each person through his unbreakable, unconditional, unfathomable love. And he offers every one of us mercy, compassion, grace, and enough strength to face whatever comes tomorrow. When we accept his love and open ourselves to his presence in our lives, he empowers us to extend that same love to everyone around us. Scripture teaches us that having the Holy Spirit living inside us profoundly transforms our interior lives, including our hearts, minds, souls. In Christ, we have been made a new creation, we have been given new affections—the love of Jesus for the world. Knowing Jesus should mean that we see other people with the eyes of Jesus.

Pause for a moment and imagine a world where empathy and understanding prevail over judgment and condemnation. What would it look like if we saw others through the eyes of Jesus, recognizing their inherent worth and humanity? How would it transform our relationships, communities, and even society in general? When we choose to extend love and acceptance to people who may be different from us, we are not only reflecting the character of Jesus but also participating in the renewal and restoration of humanity.

The modern age, with its expanded lexicon of social maladies, has made our personal judgments toward others feel objective and authoritative, but our predisposition to condemn others is not new. People have objectified others since the moment sin entered the world and the first humans turned blame to the other.

In light of this, we have to be mindful of our tendency toward self-centeredness and cultivate empathy and perspective-taking. By seeking to understand and appreciate others' experiences and emotions, we can bridge the gap that separates us and foster a more compassionate and interconnected world. This effort to see ourselves through the eyes of others allows us to reclaim the inherent subjectivity and shared humanity that lie at the heart of our relationships.

Jesus' message of love and acceptance for the other remains just as revolutionary today as it was in ancient Palestine. Society was deeply divided in the first century, with rigid hierarchies and marginalized groups, such as the poor, foreigners, women, and people with physical disabilities. Jesus challenged these societal norms, however, and emphatically proclaimed that every individual is deserving of love and respect. His teachings shattered the barriers that separated people and called for a radical shift in how we view and interact with one another. In a world that still thrives on division, his message stands clear: love knows no boundaries, and acceptance breaks down walls.

Behind Enemy Lines

Samaria, located between Galilee and Judea, presented the quickest route for travel between the two regions. Scholars believe, however, that most Jews opted for a lengthier journey along the Jordan River valley, spanning six days, to avoid interacting with Samaritans. This decision resulted in doubled time, effort, and expenses solely to evade the Samaritan people.

Contrary to the norm, Jesus chose to travel through the heart of Samaria, venturing into enemy territory to connect with people from a vastly different world. This act of nonconformity resonates with me because it highlights his resistance against stereotypes and prejudices, and his passionate love for the other. The text doesn't say that Jesus needed to use the shorter route to meet a certain deadline. It just says he "had to" go through Samaria (John 4:4).

One theory is that Jesus was under intense pressure at this point in his ministry, and people under stress do unusual things. I've done things under stress that I couldn't always rationalize, but I did them in an effort to alleviate the pressure of the moment. Back when gas was a lot cheaper, I would get into my car and just drive around the city. Mile after mile. Neighborhood after neighborhood. Suburb after suburb. Something about the freedom of the open road, a change in scenery, the rhythm of the tires on asphalt, and the mile markers steadily flying by is better than a day at the spa. Okay, maybe that's a slight exaggeration, but my point still stands. We all do unusual things under stress. But going through Samaria wouldn't have alleviated the stress Jesus was under, it would have added to it.

Perhaps the reason Jesus "had" to journey through Samaria was rooted in his unyielding commitment to fulfilling his Father's will. People driven by such profound dedication often take paths that may appear eccentric to those seeking comfort and ease. Throughout his gospel, John, Jesus' beloved disciple, paints a vivid image of a Messiah who heeds heavenly guidance, lives entirely in the present, and courageously undertakes extraordinary actions to execute his Father's intentions. This detour through Samaria could merely represent Jesus' following the Spirit's leading. If the Spirit could guide him into the wilderness for temptation by the devil, couldn't he also steer him to Samaria to minister to the Jews' antagonists? The Spirit moves freely, and above all, he seeks the renewal, restoration, and reformation of humanity.

Despite his willingness to follow the leading of the Spirit, these were not easy days for Jesus. They were a roller coaster of celebration and persecution. He was loved one day and hated the next, welcomed into one community and driven out of the following one. He left Judea because his ministry was under intense scrutiny by the Pharisees, who resented his popularity. And because these were the early days and the time had not yet come for him to confront them, he left Jerusalem, where the temple, the priests, and religious leaders were, and headed back to the sanctuary of the smaller fishing villages of Galilee.

But not until he went through Samaria.

The scandal of Jesus going where the religious community would judge him was no small matter. It's tempting for us to look back on these ancient rivalries and think, "Oh, that's nice. Jesus loved someone from across the tracks. That seems like a Jesus-y thing to do." We miss how offensive this journey would have been to the people in the religious community. And since Jesus was both fully God and fully man, we know he was capable of feeling lonely, angry, and misunderstood by the inevitable backlash that he experienced. Even though he had to follow the leading of the Spirit, that doesn't mean it didn't hurt his heart to do it.

Unfortunately, as a pastor, I've experienced firsthand

how painfully alienating it is when the tide of popular opinion turns against you based on who you associate with. And by the way—sometimes this isn't always the overlooked people of society. It has to do with the "underlooked" people, too: the rich, the celebrity, the person who has everything on the outside but feels empty within.

During the past few years, our global church was often criticized by some in the religious community over our willingness to meet people where they are. Our love for people compelled us to minister to people from all walks of life. We welcomed home the famous and the nameless. Our services were attended by celebrities, professional athletes, entertainers, social influencers, and pop icons who worshiped Jesus alongside ordinary people like me. Our vulnerable and underserved neighbors were equally welcomed and loved.

To my knowledge, no one criticized our commitment to serve the poor, but we were judged for our willingness to walk with high-profile people through their public struggles, sins, and scandals without rejecting or condemning them. We have been described pejoratively as "that celebrity church" because of our willingness to create an inclusive environment that met people where they were, on both ends of the spectrum and everywhere in between.

Why are we humans so quick to judge and attribute negative motives to things we don't understand? Why does the religious community often criticize and condemn those who are genuinely doing the work of the kingdom, simply because it doesn't fit their narrow perception of what ministry should look like? This pattern of judgment and condemnation, seen in the time of Jesus, persists. Just like the religious leaders who criticized Jesus for extending love and service to people deemed socially unacceptable, there are still those today who try to restrict and place boundaries on who we can show God's love to. Perhaps this is why Jesus felt compelled to go through Samaria, to challenge these ingrained prejudices and demonstrate that God's love is for all people, regardless of social norms or religious expectations.

Jesus had to show without a doubt and in no uncertain terms that God's love is for all people everywhere. This message was so vitally important that it couldn't be fully captured in a sermon or summed up in a parable. He knew that for his followers to understand the all-encompassing nature of God's audacious, outrageous love, he had to physically go to the one group of people that would make them question the definition of "all."

Why is the church more comfortable with some "others" and not other "others"? Whether we admit it or not, we all have a list of sins that we rank worse than others, and it correlates to how we feel about some sinners. I won't risk listing the sins that the church has found to be more heinous for fear of distracting you from the point I'm trying to make, but every generation has one or more categories of sin that rise above the others and make the Pharisees of that generation think those sins are worthy of greater condemnation.

Why do we judge each other's "Samaria"?

Each of us has our own unique mission field, our own Samaria, and it is not our place to judge or condemn where the Spirit leads others. It can be tempting to believe that our own mission field is the only valid one, and in doing so, we undermine the significance and validity of others' callings and ministries. Jesus' message of love is meant for all people, regardless of their location or circumstances. When we start discriminating and deciding who is deserving of our attention, we are falling into the same trap as the Pharisees, prioritizing our own preferences over God's overarching mission.

Jesus' eyes weren't on the acceptance of the crowds and his ears weren't attuned to the voices of popular opinion. He was looking for an open heart and a willing spirit and someone in need of hope and healing. He was looking for a woman living in the shadows of shame.

The story of this detour sends a powerful message to anyone who has ever needed Jesus to go out of his way to meet them in their mess. We do not have a Savior who shies away from the hard places. He touched lepers. He loved beggars. He ate with sinners. Jesus didn't require people to be healed, cleaned, or forgiven before they dared approach him. Instead, he went into their homes, he reached out to them in the streets, and he met them and loved them where they were, mess and all.

In a culture that was obsessed with ritual purity, these were audacious acts. In their culture, eating with someone connected you with them in a profound way; it meant you belonged to each other. Even in our culture, sharing a meal involves something deeper than the exchange of food. Fellowship is formed when someone generously serves a meal and another person gratefully receives it. Eating together is a way of identifying with each other. For the length of a meal, strangers around a table become something more: a family.

That's one of the many reasons the Pharisees were scandalized by Jesus. When he ate with sinners, Jesus was associating himself, connecting himself, *identifying* himself with them. He was extending grace and acceptance without requiring them to repent or change anything about their lives. He didn't demand that they clean themselves up before they came to him. He welcomed and loved them and shared his table with them just as they were.

The love of God compelled him, just as the love of Christ compels us.[2]

Ours is a gospel born of love, shaped by love, and commissioned in love. Love is the nature of the good news, and to the degree we follow the gospel, we, too, are born, shaped, and commissioned by love. We cannot separate the gospel from love any more than we can separate the body from breath and still call it living.

Following the example of this Savior who visits unpopular places and eats with sinners has also put me in some uncomfortable situations throughout my years in ministry. I've felt compelled to visit more than one risky place in an attempt to share his love and kindness with others. In the language of the verse describing Jesus' detour through Samaria: I *had* to visit them. From church planting in Russia immediately after the fall of the USSR, to ministering in South Africa during apartheid, to preaching in risky places in Asia and the Middle East, to marching in support of the Black community following George Floyd's murder, there are places and spaces where I have felt compelled to go. Just as I felt compelled to write this book encouraging you to interrogate your own way of being in the world.

Where do you feel compelled to go?

Who do you feel compelled to love?

What keeps you from living a life of radical kindness?

Sometimes your Samaria is a world away, sometimes it's across the street, and sometimes it is across the room you are already standing in.

Tribes versus Tribalism

It's easy to identify outsiders when we make international missions trips like the ones I've just described.[3] A few years ago, my wife and I visited an African village so remote that the children had never seen a white woman before. They gathered from neighboring communities just to see her hair and to touch her skin. She loved every moment—the smiles, the laughter, the squeals of joy, and, most of all, the opportunity to share the love of Jesus with every child. In situations like that, we have no doubt who the other is. For us, it was them. For them, it was us.

But the waters grow murky when the other is someone from our own family, church, or community. What do we do when the people we sit next to at Thanksgiving dinner, or sit next to in a church service, or sit next to in our work meetings or neighborhood gatherings turn out to be the other? It can be deeply unsettling when someone that we thought was exactly like us turns out to have different ideas about issues such as politics, sexuality, and faith. We want our tribe to be full of people who look, act, and think like we do, and losing that can feel like a threat to our very existence.

Human beings form into groups for many reasons, including security, identification, and belonging. And then, over time, we create values-based groups within those larger groups. There is nothing wrong with forming these types of bonds. It is part of human nature. Our earliest ancestors banded together for survival, and each generation has followed that same behavior. We love belonging to teams, clubs, and associations. Just watch a stadium full of fans at a college football game on a Saturday. For some people, the three words that express their greatest sense of belonging are "circle of friends."

We see a picture of such human groups at their best and worst all through the Bible. Ancient Israel was a nation of related tribes; God chose twelve to express the beauty and strength of diversity. Even Jesus was part of a tribe. He didn't enter time and space as a generic person in a generic place. He entered a context—a family, a neighborhood, a community, and a genetically bonded tribe. He was born as a Jewish man of the tribe of Judah. He had a people. He belonged somewhere.

Tribes, both literal and metaphorical, have been around since the dawn of humanity, and they are here to stay. Most of us will be a part of many such groups during our lifetimes.

The problem is not with tribes, it's with tribalism. Whereas tribes are based around common values, mutual loves, and a shared sense of history or identity, tribalism is a mindset that is not about those things at all. In our culture, a tribalistic mentality is based on opposition to anything that would seem to threaten one's group. It is grounded in exclusion and self-preservation, and it rises to destroy any perceived opposition to its existence. You are within my walls or outside them. You are on my bus or under it.

Tribalism develops when we become so entrenched in our group that we view everyone outside it with suspicion. Suspicion becomes the breeding ground for fear, and fear gives birth to hostility. If we interrogate our biases early enough in their formation, we can usually stop the progression from snowballing into outright hostility. When we fail to identify and address the issues beneath fear, we resort to destructive behaviors as a means of self-protection.

We are all connected to tribal groups. We all have a people. We all have a place. We either affirm our commitment to them or reject and replace them as we grow. Along the way, we form or join other tribes that align with our interests and affections. We join tribes when we align with a political party or decide which church to attend. We join tribes when we attend college or adopt sports teams or embrace certain ways of eating, like veganism. *Okay, maybe that's an example of tribalism!*

At their best, tribes connect us with other likeminded people, and they strengthen our commitments to a common ideal. And that can be a beautiful thing. But when we isolate ourselves within our tribes and look at members of the other tribes as objects instead of subjects, we descend into the divisive world of tribalism.

Nowhere is this more evident than in the world of tribal politics.

During the past decade I have been stunned to watch people I love and admire allow ideological and political beliefs to supplant a Christlike commitment to kindness, compassion, and civility. It is as if their identity as a conservative or a liberal trumps their identification with the Sermon on the Mount. When our commitment to our earthly groups transcends our allegiance to the way of Jesus, we have embraced idolatry, and that is the beginning of ideological tribalism. *New York Times* contributor David Brooks writes on this in his book *The Second Mountain*:

These days, partisanship for many people is not about which political party has the better policies. It's a conflict between the saved and the damned. People often use partisan identity to fill the void left when their other attachments wither away—ethnic, neighborhood, religious, communal, familial. This is asking more from politics than politics can deliver. Once politics becomes your ethnic or moral identity, it becomes impossible to compromise, because compromise becomes dishonor. Once politics becomes your identity, then every electoral contest is a struggle for existential survival, and everything is permitted.[4]

Our allegiance to the heavenly kingdom must outweigh, at all times, and in every circumstance, our fidelity to the kingdoms of this age. Despite what tribal dictates demand, as the people of God we have an identity that transcends all lesser affiliations and calls us to demonstrate kindness to those in other tribes. It's okay to be a Democrat if you can be faithful to the gospel in that political tribe. It's okay to be a Republican if you can be faithful to the gospel in that political tribe. And it's okay to be an Independent or member of the Green Party if you can be faithful to the gospel in those political tribes. But it's not okay to dehumanize and demonize one another.

To move away from this way of thinking, we have to value our relational connection with others more than we value their acceptance of our ideals. We don't have to give up our tribal distinctives to relate to or love people unlike ourselves, but we do have to be willing to look beyond them to see the people in front of us.

If anyone had the right to remain aloof from those unlike him, it was Jesus. Yet he condescended from glory in utter humility to enter our divided and suffering world. He crossed every boundary to move into the human community, and not so he could spend his days arguing with us, ridiculing us, or condemning us. Though he was perfect and sinless in every way, he did not use his divine status to make us feel as if we were the other. Instead of emphasizing the gap between his holiness and our sinfulness, he minimized the distinction. And this was not just for our salvation but also as an example of how we should be in the world. Through his life, death, and resurrection, he formed a new tribe, a new humanity, called to be completely committed to loving others before themselves.

Jesus has opened his new community to anyone and everyone who believes on his name—that he is God's Son, sent to die and raised to life for us. His tribe is the most diverse, inclusive, and welcoming tribe that has existed in the history of the world. It is one community for all people. As Patrick Miller and Keith Simon write in *Truth over Tribe*, "A healthy tribe is one that welcomes *all* people and treats outsiders with kindness, generosity, and respect. Jesus's tribe—the church—is the only tribe open to everyone. It is multi-lingual, multi-ethnic, multi-national, multi-personality, multi-perspectival, and multi-political. By joining this tribe, you can enjoy a tribal sense of belonging without animosity toward outsiders. After all, Jesus's tribe exists, in part, to serve and love *them*."[5]

Tribalism and the fear of the other will hinder our ability to love and embrace the people around us. But we have a choice. We can resist the divisive pull of tribalism and instead commit to building a community consistent with the love and grace of Jesus.

In his encounter with the woman in Samaria, Jesus shows us how to transcend the divisions in our world. It begins by seeing every person on the planet as worthy of love and respect. It means looking deep enough within them to bear witness to the residue of the divine, despite how faint it may appear. It involves looking for the things we hold in common, starting with the shared longings of every human heart to find acceptance, meaning, and significance. And it means giving up our tendency to disparage them, despite how much we may disagree with them. We can win arguments, or we can win people, but we cannot do both.

chapter 3

separation of church and hate

religion, oppression, and safe havens

So he came to a town in Samaria called Sychar, near the plot of ground Jacob had given to his son Joseph. Jacob's well was there, and Jesus, tired as he was from the journey, sat down by the well. It was about noon.
—John 4:5–6

Recently, my wife and I journeyed to the Deep South to spend a few days with our extended family. When I refer to the Deep South, I'm speaking of what locals affectionately call the "dirty, dirty South." (For anyone north of the Mason-Dixon line, that's an expression of fondness.) Our trip was a family reunion of sorts, as we hadn't seen some relatives in quite a while. Our trip included time in New Orleans (N'awlins), where we revisited some cherished memories from our dating days, drove an hour north to the site of our wedding, stopped by our first apartment, and concluded in the heart of Louisiana. This gathering was particularly special; it marked the first time my parents and all three of us siblings had been together in two decades. For much of that time, my younger brother had been deployed with the military in various parts of the globe. On the flight back to Phoenix, I realized how little I knew about our family history. Inspired by this realization, I did something I've thought about doing for the past couple of years: I visited Ancestry.com. After signing up for their service, I paid the fee and hit the Enter key, then sat back and waited.

And waited.

And waited.

I soon realized that my expectations for the site had been a little unrealistic. I thought you could type in a couple of names, hit Enter, then watch your family tree magically form before your eyes, like something out of *CSI*, with all the little pixels slowly coming into place. And what I discovered is that *you* have to do all the work. *It's embarrassing to write that, but it's true.*

The nerve! Even after paying the fee, they expect you to go out there and hunt down your relatives the old-fashioned way. You must look at online obituary columns, birth records, and online newspaper clippings. You must go to creepy websites where you look at old graves. And you must search through archives.

What?! Who has time for that? I just wanted to hit a button and get some immediate answers.

So I called my sister-in-law. That's what we do when we can't fix stuff at our house—we call my wife's sister Jill. Jill came to live with us just after our first son was born. He had some special needs and she wanted to assist our family, so she came to visit and stayed for eighteen years! It takes someone special to make that kind of commitment, and she is that kind of person. Jill is as much a part of our immediate family as our kids are, but even better, she can fix stuff! I discovered she had an account on Ancestry.com and, in researching my wife's family tree, had pieced together some of my own.

It wasn't long before I discovered that if my family tree were an actual tree, it would be desperately in need of pruning. Regardless of who you are and what beautiful illusions you hold about the sanctity of your family history, your family tree always looks better at a distance.

Trust me.

I thought my family tree would be filled with noble and virtuous people. I expected to find pastors and leaders, teachers and farmers, nurses and abolitionists. I thought my family would be the bedrock of the community. And there were a few people who fit that category—right alongside the outlaws and the bandits. It has been both exciting and distressing to see my family tree.

One of the most important lessons I've learned through the process is that backstories matter.

Have you ever wondered why God included the painful backstories of some of his most faithful followers in the Bible? Wouldn't it have been better for us all to let history omit Noah's drunkenness or Moses' cowardice or David's affair? It would have created a much better image for faith if the world weren't aware of these enormous failures.

Perhaps there's a deeper purpose in these painful places. God doesn't hide the messy backstories in our spiritual family tree. Instead, he treats them as the ongoing chapters in his story of full and complete redemption. As the Author and Finisher of our faith, he writes each of our stories with careful consideration, composing every sentence with meticulous care. He doesn't write first drafts, redrafts, or wasted drafts. His chapters are never awash in a sea of red ink, indicating their need for revision. Instead, he writes our storylines, and as we drift, sin, repent, and return, he incorporates new mercies and fresh starts, allowing everyone to see where we come from and what we've overcome. Ultimately, the final composition is beyond what we could have ever anticipated. It is a story marked by grace and the faithfulness of our God. How God can redeem our painful backstories and include all of us in his masterpiece is beyond comprehension.

God is infinitely more concerned with making sure we know how much we are chosen, loved, and sought after than he is with trying to make us look impressive in the eyes of the world. The world judges and defines us by the images we project, but God views us as his beloved children, despite how many ups and downs and twists and turns our storylines have.

These real and raw biblical stories display God's kindness, compassion, and willingness to enter into the messiness of our story. He meets us where we are without throwing us a towel to clean ourselves first. The storied lives of the biblical elite reveal a God who isn't afraid of his people's shocking capacity for complete and utter failure. He has seen it all before, and inevitably, he will see it all again. Every one of us has something painful hidden in our past. Yet God loves each of us equally.

Unconditionally.

Irrevocably.

No one reaches the present moment without a backstory. Our individual narratives are rooted in personal experiences and events that may stretch back generations. The understanding of our personal histories, family legacies, and community origins helps us comprehend the context of our current situation. The Samaritan people entered the New Testament narrative with a rich and complex backstory. The Samaritan woman who met Jesus at the well brought her unique history to that encounter. And the very location of their meeting, the town of Shechem, had its own significant backstory, steeped in tradition and ancient history.

The Backstory of Shechem

The city of Shechem features prominently in the stories of Abraham, Jacob, and Joshua. It is the site of both communion with God and his people's worst sins. And it has a lot to teach us about the state of our holy places today.

When Abraham left his father's house in Harran and set out for the land of Canaan, the first place he camped was at the oak of Moreh, outside the city of Shechem. It was there that God appeared to him and promised he would give this land to Abraham's offspring, even though the Canaanites occupied the area at the time. He built an altar there to commemorate

God's promises before journeying on. For Abraham and his descendants, this altar outside Shechem would have been a reminder that one day this pagan land would be God's holy land.

Two generations later, when Abraham's grandson Jacob returned from his uncle's land and reconciled with his brother, Esau, he moved to a plot of land outside Shechem, which he bought from the pagan king of Shechem, Hamor. Jacob also built an altar there called El Elohe Israel, meaning "Mighty is the God of Israel." Jacob most likely settled there because its location in the promised land at the crossroads of trade made it a convenient choice.

Unfortunately, this place where Jacob moved his family and built an altar did not turn out to be a sacred place for his family. This story should come with trigger warnings. Dinah, the daughter of Jacob and Leah, went out to visit her friends in the city, and the prince of Shechem, also named Shechem, noticed her, took her by force, and raped her. Then, still not satisfied with stealing her innocence, he asked his father, Hamor, king of Shechem, to broker a deal with Jacob to make her his wife. Suddenly this place was no longer a refuge for a wanderer or a site to encounter God but rather a place of fear, intimidation, and abuse.

Dinah's experience is not isolated. Countless women across generations have encountered similar situations in places they believed to be safe. Despite the passage of time, human behavior remains tragically unchanged, and sinful and predatory tendencies continue to manifest. In late 2017, the #MeToo movement gained widespread attention when revelations of almost three decades of sexual misconduct by film producer Harvey Weinstein came to light. Woman after woman shared her story of abuse at the hands of influential men. This wave of honesty and courage soon reached faith communities, giving rise to the #churchtoo hashtag. It served as a poignant reminder that sexual abuse can and does lurk in even the most unlikely and sacred spaces.

What evil have we allowed to creep into our sacred and holy spaces?

Jacob's initial response to his daughter's rape is eerily similar to how many influential men in the church have responded to sexual abuse allegations: he did nothing. He was silent in the face of evil. He did not rush to his daughter's side to comfort and protect her. He did not demand justice. He did not bring this evil out in the open but instead kept silent. Jacob was supposed to be a man of God. The man of God in his generation—the God of Abraham, Isaac, and *Jacob*. The nation of Israel would even be named after him. Yet he did nothing to defend the honor of his own daughter.

Silence is not kindness.

As we have heard chanted in the streets of our cities, there is a time when silence is violence. Consider the role of silence in your own life and community. Are there times when you have remained silent in the face of injustice or abuse? Moving forward, how can you promote a culture of accountability and speak up for those who have been victimized?

Jacob's second response was equally as disturbing and similar to what we have seen happen in many churches. He met with Shechem and his father to arrange Dinah's marriage to the man who raped her. *Why would any loving father do this?*

The text tells us exactly why and it *is* deeply disturbing. Hamor promised Jacob an alliance. If he gave Dinah to Shechem in marriage, all of their children could intermarry and the whole city of Shechem would be open to them, not just the land they had bought on the outskirts of town. They could freely live and trade in the city and buy property there. Jacob traded his daughter's dignity for a business deal. Just like so many men in powerful positions have done to vulnerable young women who were abused in their churches.

Dinah's brothers were furious at what their father was doing. In response, they tricked Shechem, his father, and all the men of the area into getting circumcised as a requirement of the marriage deal. When they were weak from the surgery, Dinah's brothers Simeon and Levi killed all the men of the city to avenge their sister's rape. Then, in some ironic twisted morality, they continued the cycle of violence against women by carting off their women and children.

Jacob may have thought that standing up to Hamor and defending his daughter would have cost him everything, but his silence led to even more violence and abuse. That is the nature of sin; the things we hide grow until they can't be hidden any longer.

Once again, Jacob's final response to this mounting crisis is an uncanny echo of the church's reaction to abuse today. He got angry, not at the fact that his daughter was violated but at the disgrace that the whole situation brought upon himself. He was furious with his sons that now the other pagan people of the land could turn against them in battle. Jacob's reactions to his daughter's rape read like a playbook that generations of men after him have followed when a woman is victimized: silence, cover-ups, and backdoor deals, blaming the victim and clinging to power instead of reaching out to help the powerless.

Thousands of years later, we find ourselves still startled by emerging reports of large Christian institutions mishandling abuse cases, prioritizing the reputation of the church over the well-being of women, and obstructing justice for victims. Influential figures, often revered as "men of God," from the days of Jacob to the present, have exploited their authority to conceal wrongdoing and silence victims. Instead of investing in the challenging work to confront evil, unveil the truth, and establish measures to prevent ongoing and future abuse, they have chosen the path of evasion and concealment. Cover-ups are destructive to the core.

Faith communities become spiritually toxic when we fail to safeguard them from this kind of abuse. What happened at Shechem happens in institutions and churches when we don't hold ourselves and others accountable to a commitment to protect the innocent, the vulnerable, and those who have been entrusted to our spiritual care. While this chapter focuses on violence against women, it is important to note that men are also abused, and this protection should extend to every person who walks through the doors of our churches.

A few chapters later in Genesis, Shechem becomes the place where Joseph was sold into slavery by his brothers. Shechem has become the site of rape, misogyny, mass murder, idolatry, and human trafficking, and although this community appears to be beyond the hope of rescue, nothing—no person, no place, no situation—is ever beyond redemption.

Many generations later, after more than four hundred

years of slavery in Egypt and forty years of wandering in the wilderness, Joshua assembled a new generation of Israelites at Shechem to renew the covenant before they entered the promised land and to offer them the choice between serving the God of Abraham or serving their false gods. The first generation of Israelites to come out of slavery in Egypt had wandered in the desert for forty years, trying to become the holy people God called them to be and failing at nearly every turn. During their wanderings, they had clung to the gods of the Egyptians and even picked up new gods along the way. Sin had run rampant among them, but this was a new generation, with a new hope that they would enter the promised land and live with God as his holy people.

As they stood on the threshold of the promised land, Joshua gathered all the tribes and together they committed to rid themselves of all foreign gods. He then led them to Shechem, where God promised to give the land to Abraham and his descendants. Despite its sordid history, God chose Shechem as the place for this renewal, the fulfillment of his promises, and a beacon of hope for the future.[1]

This was a moment of reckoning.

This new generation of Israelites had the option to continue covering up their sin or to acknowledge the evil among them. They could protect the status quo or stand up to the existing power structures. They could reinforce shameful, degrading behaviors or put in the hard and holy work that leads to human flourishing.

Our church and religious institutions face the same reckoning today. As more and more stories of abuse surface, perpetrated by spiritual leaders, and covered up by defenders of religious institutions, the choice is clear. We can double down in defiance and surrender to the fear that this reckoning will destroy the church, or we can humble ourselves before the people we've been called to protect, acknowledge the sin we have allowed to metastasize, and repent of our ways.

Can we be the generation that finally puts a stop to abuse and cover-ups, and embrace our calling to live as God's holy people in the world? If we trust in God's profound love for his church, and his commitment to see her adorned as a holy and spotless bride, we need not fear this moment of shaking and remaking. It will not destroy us; rather, it will refine and purify us. Only then will the church's witness be restored in the eyes of a watching and waiting world. This reckoning will lead us to repentance, ushering in the cool winds of refreshing and renewal and opening the door to a new beginning. And so it was that Shechem, that terrible, tainted place, became the site where the Israelites renewed their covenant with God. It was there that the Israelites acknowledged their sin, threw away their foreign gods, and yielded their hearts to the Lord.[2] They recommitted themselves to following God's ways and were finally ready to inhabit the promised land.

The Jews of Jesus' time knew all about Shechem's painful backstory. Just its name would have grabbed their attention and put them on alert for another terrible event to happen there. Imagine, then, the disciples' surprise when Jesus announced that Shechem was next on the itinerary. Perhaps they wondered if Jesus would finally call down fire and brimstone and wipe that godforsaken place off the map. But that wasn't what he had in mind.

Jesus sat at the place where Dinah was raped, where Jacob

cowered, and where Joseph was betrayed, and he opened his heart to a woman who symbolized all of that historical pain and suffering. Is it possible that this moment was about not just the salvation of a woman and her community but also the redemption of this place? Does Jesus redeem only individuals or does his redemption extend to communities, places, and spaces? Does he care only about people or does he care for gated communities, high-rise buildings, neighborhoods, and housing projects? What about suburbs, cities, rural areas, and villages, like Shechem?

What can we learn from Jacob's silence and failure to defend his daughter Dinah, and how it seems to mirror the faith community's historical mishandling of abuse cases?

The biblical story of Shechem and its painful back-story challenge our understanding of sacred spaces and the church's role in addressing abuse and oppression. It calls us to question how we have mirrored Jacob's silence and failure to defend the vulnerable and how we have mishandled abuse cases throughout history. As we grapple with these questions, we are compelled to confront how we have operated within our sacred institutions and seek a new way forward—a way that embraces justice, compassion, and the healing of the wounded.

Jesus' encounter with the woman from Shechem defied every expectation and revealed a powerful juxtaposition to the story of Dinah and Jacob. While Jacob remained silent and failed to defend his daughter, Jesus spoke up and demonstrated compassion and empathy. Jacob ignored Dinah, but Jesus asked questions, listened closely, and offered affirmations to the victimized woman at the well. In the aftermath,

Jacob's sons carried out a devastating act of violence, while the people of the village in the story of the woman at the well were saved. These contrasting responses prompt us to reflect on Jacob's silence and failure to protect Dinah and how it echoes the historical mishandling of abuse cases within the faith community.

Wells and Weddings

Does it seem sacrilegious to imagine Jesus as the bridegroom proposing marriage to the Samaritan woman at the well? It wasn't for Saint Augustine, who saw the Samaritan woman as a representation of the bride of Christ. Augustine, the fourth-century bishop of Hippo, wrote, "It is pertinent to the image of the reality that this [Samaritan] woman, who bore the type of the church, comes from strangers, for the church was to come from the Gentiles, an alien race of the Jews."[3]

In his extraordinary work *Jesus the Bridegroom: The Greatest Love Story Ever Told*, Brant Pitre writes, "As many scholars have recognized, from an ancient Jewish perspective the Samaritan woman looks suspiciously like a potential bride. Although it's easy for modern readers to miss this point entirely, the similarities would have been a lot clearer for ancient Jewish readers of John's account. They would have been privy to one key piece of cultural information: at the time of Jesus, if you were an eligible young Jewish man looking for an eligible young Jewish woman, you would not go to a bar or to a club. Instead, you would go where the ladies were to be found: the local well."[4]

In that part of the world, wells were *the* gathering place in a community and were often situated in central locations, sort of like a coffee shop on the busiest street in town. They were known not only as the ideal places to get engaged but also, oddly enough, as sites to seek divine revelation. I can't think of a modern equivalent for an ancient well apart from imagining a quaint wedding chapel with a lush garden suddenly springing up in your local Starbucks. There is one thing I can imagine quite clearly, though, because we see it throughout Scripture: wells are places where God mediated divine purposes. He seeks people out at wells. He meets with them at wells. And he transforms lives and communities at wells.

Wells are one of the places where God joins people in their stories.

Reflecting on the significance of wells in Jesus' time challenges us to consider the broader implications for our lives and communities. How can we create spaces and places where people are receptive to having God join them in their stories? How can we create spaces where people are truly seen and loved? How can we foster the kind of environments that awaken the longings of the heart to know and be known by God? In another story in the Old Testament, God met with a woman at a spring of water away from her community, in her time of need, in the same way that Jesus met with the woman at the well in Samaria. This woman was Hagar, who was an enslaved Egyptian and Abraham and Sarai's servant and surrogate. When Hagar fled Sarai's mistreatment, the angel of the Lord appeared to her at a well and conveyed a divine message about her son, Ishmael, and his plan for her many descendants. Following that encounter, she called the Lord "the One who sees me," and the well was named "the well of the Living One who sees me." Even though the father and mother of our faith had mistreated and rejected her, God still acknowledged her. He sent an angel into the desert to meet her, comfort her, and assure her that she was seen and valued in his eyes, foreshadowing Jesus' interaction with the woman at the well in Samaria.

Later, when Hagar was finally sent away by Abraham and Sarah, she and her son found themselves alone in the desert, out of water and frightened they would die of thirst. As the relentless desert sun beat down, Hagar's hope dwindled to a whisper, and she sobbed in despair, her tears mixing with the dry sand. God, attuned to the suffering of the forsaken, heard Ishmael's plaintive cries echoing in the wilderness and spoke to Hagar audibly, his voice a calming presence. The God who had seen her, who had observed her struggle and pain, now also heard her son's desperate plea. God reassured and comforted her with warm, compassionate words, then guided her eyes to a well nearby, its water shimmering under the hot sun, providing them with life-sustaining nourishment when death seemed but a heartbeat away.[5]

Similarly, when Jesus encountered the Samaritan woman, he offered her something beyond physical sustenance: the promise of eternal life. Just as God had opened Hagar's eyes to a well that saved her life, Jesus revealed to the Samaritan woman a "spring of water welling up to eternal life."[6]

Wells are more than just sites of divine revelation; they are also iconic settings for romance. In the Bible, three notable couples began their love stories at a well: Isaac and Rebekah, Jacob and Rachel, and Moses and Zipporah.

Isaac and Rebekah's betrothal unfolded through the

devoted prayer of Abraham's servant, Eleazar. Charged to find a suitable wife for Isaac, Eleazar approached a well outside the village just as evening descended, the time when women came to draw water. Filled with hope and expectation, he prayed to God for guidance, seeking a specific sign: if a woman not only gave him a drink but also offered to water his camels, she would be the one destined for Isaac. Rebekah responded as he had hoped, leading to her engagement to Isaac. In this sacred moment at the well, a divine revelation was granted, and the initial steps were taken toward a union that would influence the destiny of an entire people. The convergence of the sacred and the ordinary at the well framed a love story guided by faith, exemplifying both heavenly revelation and earthly romance.[7]

Even more important, given his later prominence, Isaac's son Jacob also encountered romance and revelation at a well. While journeying to stay with his uncle Laban, Jacob paused at a well in the region and observed Rachel coming to water her father's sheep. Their meeting was not by mere chance; it was a destined encounter. Moved deeply by her beauty and profound gratitude for God's faithfulness, Jacob approached her, watered the sheep, and then kissed her cheeks as a sign of greeting. At that moment, by the well, a lifelong love affair was kindled, weaving together love and providence. This was the very same well where Jesus later encountered the Samaritan woman.

The third romance situated by a well unfolded when Moses fled Egypt to escape Pharaoh's wrath after defending a Hebrew slave. He sought refuge in Midian and found himself at a well where he encountered seven sisters, all struggling with other shepherds for access to water their father's flock. Driven by a sense of justice and compassion, Moses intervened, securing the water and tending to the sheep. Impressed by his kindness and bravery, their father welcomed Moses into his home and offered his daughter Zipporah's hand in marriage. This encounter at the well transformed a moment of conflict into an opportunity for love and family, once again illustrating the transformative power that wells held in the tapestry of biblical narratives.

The ancient Jews would have known these stories intimately, perhaps even more than we know the familial love stories of our parents and grandparents. They would have recognized the recurring pattern in these ancient romantic narratives, akin to a divine formula: man + woman + well = marriage. This motif, far from being merely a literary device, resonated throughout their culture, symbolizing a union orchestrated by divine providence.

The Unlovables

Fifteen years ago, when my sister-in-law began a relationship with an African American man in our congregation, it caused rifts within our extended family and even in the church community. The same young lady who researched my family's genealogy, the one who came to help our family when our son was born and was our rock in so many ways, experienced a lot of rejection for falling in love with someone who didn't share the same skin color. It's disappointing to acknowledge that some members of our extended family even refused to attend their wedding.

Aware of our inclination to label, judge, and exclude one another, Jesus sets the stage for a symbolic betrothal with a Samaritan woman at a well. This act was a prophetic statement against the prejudices of his time. Instead of proposing an earthly marriage, Jesus was introducing something more profound: a spiritual betrothal. The Samaritan woman was no ordinary bachelorette. Being a Samaritan—a blend of Israelite and gentile—she was an unlikely choice, particularly in the eyes of religious leaders of her time, for a young Jewish bachelor like Jesus to pursue, if this were a tale of earthly romance. Yet the spiritual symbolism of the story unveils God's intention to bring together Jew and gentile, forming them into the church, the very bride of Christ.

Though her complicated marital history seemed to disqualify her in the eyes of society, Jesus looked beyond these earthly imperfections. Her shortcomings, rather than hindering her, made her a fitting recipient of his radical kindness. In the same way, our imperfections do not disqualify us but rather position us to receive his kindness and compassion.

The narrative provides subtle clues about the Samaritan woman's age. The fact that she had been married five times suggests she was likely older, possibly even older than Jesus. While her age might have been perceived as yet another barrier in her society, it is beautifully transcended within the context of this story. This subtle detail serves as a powerful reminder that, in the realm of faith and grace, conventional barriers and societal judgments lose their significance, giving way to a more profound understanding of worth and value. The encounter between Jesus and the Samaritan woman stands as more than a historical footnote; it embodies a divine movement, a sweeping motion that opens the gates of redemption to people of all nations. Within what might appear to be an ordinary interaction, God unveils a timeless portrait of his inexhaustible kindness and compassion. Through this conversation, he conveys his desire to redeem every single one of us, regardless of skin color, tribe, culture, or painful backstory. The message is clear: we are all welcome at the well.

Spiritual Wells

What if we envisioned our churches as communal wells where Jesus would feel welcome to sit and engage in meaningful conversations, and where even those without faith can freely participate in thoughtful dialogue? Tragically, this vision seems distant from our reality. Instead of building bridges, we erect barriers; instead of dialogue, we engage in hostility; instead of finding common ground, we deepen our divides; instead of healing the broken, we assign blame; instead of uncovering truth, we conceal sin, allowing it to corrode our integrity. Observing the strife within the evangelical community, I can't help but wonder: When did something so beautiful become marred by such ugliness? *Where is the church that Jesus formed to be a safe harbor for hurting and broken people?*

The church, once a shining beacon of hope, has become a source of disillusionment for many. Leaders have failed to uphold the virtues of our faith, and the "beloved community," beautifully described by Martin Luther King Jr., has been tarnished, ridiculed, and despised—not for standing for righteousness' sake but for failing to embody the values it professes.

What is the outcome of this reckoning? Martin Luther

King Jr. reminds us that "the end is reconciliation; the end is redemption; the end is the creation of the beloved community. It is this type of spirit and this type of love that can transform opposers into friends. It is this type of understanding goodwill that will transform the deep gloom of the old age into the exuberant gladness of the new age. It is this love which will bring about miracles in the hearts of men."[8]

In this season of reflection, a horizon of possibility arises— the opportunity to renew the heart and soul of the church. This can become our story if we incline our hearts toward honesty, humility, and genuine repentance. These virtues will work together to create safe havens for those who have been hurt by our actions or our absence. If we seize this moment with urgency, we can reshape the narrative of our faith in the eyes of the world, making it a beacon of love and healing once again. We must act quickly. Our window of opportunity is passing.

chapter 4

natural-born label makers

descriptions don't have to define us

When a Samaritan woman came to draw water, Jesus said to her, "Will you give me a drink?" (His disciples had gone into the town to buy food.) The Samaritan woman said to him, "You are a Jew, and I am a Samaritan woman. How can you ask me for a drink?" (For Jews do not associate with Samaritans.)
—John 4:7–9

During my childhood years, my parents possessed one of those early Avery model 68 label makers—an exquisite piece of technology in the late '60s.[1] My mother, captivated by this ingenious contraption, embarked on a labeling frenzy during the first few weeks of owning it.

Looking back, I now realize she marked things that didn't need labeling, like "knives and forks." We may not have been the brightest kids, and we could have easily opened the drawer to see what was inside, but she wanted us to know. It wasn't long before my younger brother and I, being the unholy preacher's kids that we were, sneaked the label maker out of the drawer labeled "label maker," typed inappropriate things on it, printed them off, and stuck them on people's backs.

Don't judge me.

Every bad thing I learned came from other church kids.

Reflecting on our mischievous behavior, I can see that most of our labels were relatively harmless. We typed things like "Dummy," "Weirdo," "Doo-doo head." Little did I realize my behavior was connected to a much more painful reality that I would face later in life.

As human beings, we love to label people.

And it's not just the world around us that uses these labels. When I was a kid, running around labeling people (literally), and my dad was a young pastor, the religious world had its own set of labels for pastors who preached love, kindness, and grace. Those labels were the kiss of death for anyone trying to build a ministry rooted in biblical faithfulness. They labeled them "Liberal," "Worldly," "Permissive." Today, the pejorative terms are "Woke," "Progressive," or even "Marxist."

Those old labels were sticky, and when you peeled the label off, it always left a gummy residue behind. Especially when it had been on for a while. Over the years, we had things in our house that lost their labels but you could still tell where the label used to be, because it left that shadowy reminder.

Isn't the same true for us? Throughout our lives, people

attach labels to us, which reflect and affect how others think about our identities and how we feel about ourselves. Labels are not always negative; they can reflect positive characteristics and define us in flattering ways. Who doesn't want to be called an athlete? Often, however, the labels we use to describe one another result from unfounded assumptions and negative stereotypes. We often assign them hastily and effortlessly, but once attached, they can leave behind a persistent residue on the soul, acting as a sticky reminder of how we were once defined. For good or bad, labels represent an influence on our identity that is beyond our control.

Have you ever considered how labeling others affects their individuality and how they are perceived? What if we chose to approach others without preconceived labels, assumptions, or stereotypes? How would it change our interactions and relationships? Imagine a world where we prioritize getting to know people beyond their labels. How would this transform our sense of community and foster a kinder and more gracious society?

So why do we label others?

What compels us to categorize people based on race, religious affiliation, political association, or socioeconomic status? Is it because it's an easier way of understanding them? Is it because it's more efficient to make snap judgments about who they are instead of taking the time to do the hard and holy work of getting to know them? Is it because who they are might challenge what we believe to be true about certain groups of people in general? Is it just easier to put ourselves and others into categories?

Yes.

It's all those things and more.

We resort to labeling when we lack the cognitive tools to handle complex realities. If our minds are overwhelmed with information, they default to our preconceived ideas about who other people are and how they will behave. There are almost two hundred different types of bias for our brains to choose from. And each one influences how we see, perceive, and interact with other people. These biases are based on stereotypes, prejudices, or even our past experiences with specific individuals who come to represent an entire category of people.

Most of these biases can be categorized as conscious or unconscious, otherwise described as explicit or implicit. Conscious, or explicit, biases are prejudices that allow us to discriminate against others. More often than not, they are apparent to us and those around us, like when someone is openly racist. On the other hand, unconscious, or implicit, biases are much more challenging to identify. We are often unaware of how they influence our behavior toward others. Identifying them requires a serious commitment to self-work in light of the gospel and the promise of the new creation.

A Warning Label

The Danish philosopher and theologian Søren Kierkegaard writes, "Once you label me, you negate me."[2] When an individual is labeled and then attempts to live up to (or down to) that label, it alters their essential identity. The label becomes a replacement for their true self. The people we label end up confined to our perceptions of them, and their unique individuality ceases to exist. Even worse, labeling people locks them into how we see them in any given moment, and that is a disservice to the ongoing work of grace in their lives. Even if they change and grow out of those labels, people still see them that way. And our labels can become like self-fulfilling prophecies that give form and expression to what we see.

Do you remember back in 2015 when "the dress" broke the internet? The Roman Originals dress was photographed by a woman who planned to wear it to her daughter's wedding. After some disagreement developed among her friends over the color of the dress, she uploaded the picture to Facebook. Within a week, it had been viewed more than ten million times. Some people saw the dress as black and blue and others as white and gold, which became the source of heated arguments worldwide. Apparently, we do not all see color the same. Who knew? It took science a couple of years to figure out that we each perceive color differently based on our perception of the lighting.

The more significant revelation from the controversy relates to our natural-born tendency to label those who see things differently than we do as ignorant, hateful, combative, or irrational. We believe what we see with our eyes more than we trust what others tell us, even when they are sharing verifiable facts. Over time, our brains cut and paste our perceptions, creating a confirmation bias. Our brains are our built-in, factory-made label makers.

Labels often say more about the one labeling than the one being labeled. Toni Morrison, the acclaimed Pulitzer Prize and Nobel Prize winner, once wrote that "definitions belonged to the definers—not the defined."[3] Each time we label others with the intent of defining and limiting them, we inadvertently restrict our perceptions.

The power of labels goes beyond classifying dress colors or categorizing people; labels can even shape our interpretation of complex situations. This was demonstrated in a thought-provoking study conducted at Stanford University.

Social psychologist Jennifer Eberhardt and her team at Stanford conducted an eye-opening experiment with white college students. They were presented with images of a man whose racial appearance was ambiguous and could have been classified as either white or Black. The students were divided into two groups: one group was told the face belonged to a white man, and the other was told it belonged to a Black man. Both groups were then asked to draw the face.

Even though all participants were looking at the same image, those who were inclined to believe that race is a binary category instead of a continuum drew faces that aligned more with racial stereotypes corresponding to the label they were given. The racial label effectively became a filter, shaping how they perceived and represented the individual in the image, and they couldn't separate the label from the face they were drawing.[4]

This phenomenon of labels influencing perception isn't restricted to race. In a well-known study conducted by researchers John Darley and Paget Gross, college students were shown a video of a young girl named Hannah. They were asked to evaluate her academic ability based on her responses to test questions, which varied in difficulty.

The students also received information about Hannah's background. Some were shown Hannah playing in a low-income area, with her parents described as blue-collar high-school graduates; others saw her playing in a middle-class neighborhood, with her parents portrayed as college-educated professionals.

The way Hannah was labeled, as either poor or middle class, significantly influenced the students' assessment of her academic ability. When she was considered middle class, they believed her performance was near fifth-grade level, but when she was labeled poor, they assessed her performance as below fourth-grade level.

These studies illustrate the powerful and often subconscious effect that labels, whether they relate to race or socioeconomic status, can have on our perceptions and judgments.[5] The implications of labeling are not confined to the findings of these specific studies; they reach into the broader spectrum of human interaction and understanding. The power of a label to shape perceptions is universal, affecting people across different cultures, backgrounds, and contexts. This subtle yet profound influence underscores the need for awareness and thoughtful consideration in how we categorize and define others.

During his life and ministry, Jesus bore the weight of many unjust labels and accusations. He was wrongfully characterized as a drunkard, a glutton, a madman, a demoniac, and even as a Samaritan. It is conceivable that questions surrounding his birth lingered, and he likely faced the stigma associated with being labeled as illegitimate.

Many find it easier to label Jesus than to follow him. The religious elite of his day made assumptions about him based on the company he kept, quickly leaping to label him a sinner.

They made the huge leap from "he is a friend of sinners" to "he *is* a sinner." Yet Jesus did not fear guilt by association; instead, he chose to enter our broken world, robing himself in human flesh, to redeem us. He allowed himself to be "numbered with the transgressors" rather than align with the rich and powerful. This cognitive bias, the idea of guilt by association, seems outlandish when applied to Jesus, but it continues to plague our culture and churches. We often label others guilty of sin based on their associations or deviations from strict norms. Tragically, this can lead to a point where fear of being associated with an idea outweighs our desire to love those who hold that belief.[6]

During my time as a Bible college student, I had an experience that exposed me to the reality of guilt by association. As an insider, I found myself falling in love with someone who was considered an outsider in our religious community.

Based on her religious lineage, Judith Williams should have been queen of the insiders. Her family had made significant contributions within our denomination: her paternal grandfather founded our first Bible college, her maternal grandfather served in the hierarchy, and her uncle pastored one of our most influential churches. These contributions had been overshadowed, however, by her father's and uncle's public moral failures. Times had changed, and her family's reputation was tarnished. Which meant she was labeled, and consequently, I was labeled by association. Neither of us had played any part in the scandal, but label makers usually don't care about the collateral damage, do they?

Judith had no interest in being an insider, anyway. She was passionate about serving hurting people, and she was in

Bible college only to learn how to minister to them more effectively. It was all that mattered. I had a lot to learn from her. And I'm grateful that God brought us together.

I had another experience at Bible college that didn't involve guilt by association. I actually was guilty. The fundamentalist college I attended had a list of prohibited behaviors that was as long and detailed as the book of Leviticus, one of which was going to the movies.

Did I mention that I am equal parts rule-keeper and rule-breaker?

Like most people, I enjoy keeping the rules I make and breaking the ones created by others.

The problem wasn't just that I broke the rules and attended a movie. I attended an R-rated movie instead of attending the midweek service. My transgression was so unique and multifaceted that it defied their classifications. In their minds it seemed so egregious that it might have warranted an additional tier to Dante's nine circles of hell. The confusion and disbelief were palpable on the faces of the student ministerial association council; they appeared bewildered, utterly taken aback, and at a loss for words.

They nervously adjusted their ties and their voices cracked as they interrogated me, trying to understand how someone with such a bright future as a promising young pharisee could throw it all away at "the movie picture."

Two years later, I stood before denominational officials to interview for licensure. The district board rigorously questioned me about my knowledge of Scripture, denominational history, polity, and the lapse in judgment during college. After an intense hour of deliberation, they granted me a ministerial license, accompanied by a stern warning to avoid worldly entertainment. Another two years passed, and I encountered a revelation of God's grace at a nondenominational Bible conference. It was there that I realized the extent of the legalism embedded in our denomination's man-made rules. While our denomination clung to the security of the law, I had glimpsed the wonders of forgiveness, freedom, and a righteousness grounded in the work of the cross. This awakening inspired me to return my ministerial license and follow Jesus into the uncharted realms of faith. I had tasted grace, and my soul would accept nothing less.

When I returned my credentials, I strove to be as gracious and honorable as possible, and I was taken aback when the district superintendent affirmed my decision. He seemed to sincerely desire what was best for me, saying, "I know this is hard, but this is right for you. God has something broader for you that will make a bigger impact on the world." Then, almost as an afterthought, with a twinkle in his voice, he added, "The *only* reason we credentialed you in the first place was because another college student faced charges for inappropriate behavior, and his misconduct was worse than yours. After disciplining him, we chose to show some mercy and approve you." I don't think God grades on the curve, but denominations occasionally do.

A Comparative Study

Christians have a long history of labeling other people.

This behavior stretches all the way back to biblical times and is vividly illustrated by the contrasting depictions of two women in the gospel of John: the woman at the well and the woman caught in adultery. The former was able to blend into the community, her transgressions concealed, while the latter remained hidden away in her home. One was wrongfully branded as an adulteress, whereas the other openly acknowledged her guilt. One was met with kindness and compassion, the other faced judgmental exposure. These striking contrasts create a compelling study, yet despite their distinct differences, both individuals are simply referred to as "woman."

We don't even know their names.

The first is identified as a "Samaritan woman" three times. She was a minority woman in a male-dominated, patriarchal society, and she would have been accustomed to living under one layer of prejudice after another. In a charitable effort to redeem her image and offer her some posthumous dignity, the early church christened her Photine, "the enlightened one."

The heading in my Bible identifies the second woman in this comparison as "a woman caught in adultery." This label remains affixed to her two millennia later, overshadowing any other characteristics she may have had. Perhaps she was a skilled cook, a remarkably funny person, a wise money manager, or a caregiver especially good with small children; we know none of this. We see only her label: adulteress.

This story takes place four chapters after Jesus encountered the woman at the well. He was teaching in the temple courts when the Pharisees and teachers produced a woman caught in the act of adultery. They made her stand before the crowd and used her predicament as a trap for Jesus, asking him if they should adhere to the law of Moses and stone her.

Even without knowing the full story, it's clear this was a

dreadful day for the woman involved. She was caught in a scandalous act and paraded in front of a crowd, possibly only partially clad and likely overwhelmed with shame.

Perhaps you've experienced a similar nightmare. It might have taken place at work or school, but for me, it's our largest church service on Sunday morning. In this dream, I'm standing before the congregation, but no one will make eye contact with me. Even my wife looks away. Our staff seems strangely fixated on their shoes, their faces screaming, "What is he doing?" Then a chilling sensation, like a gentle breeze, brushes against places usually protected by multiple layers of clothing (if you catch my drift). I glance down, realizing that it's not my sermon I've forgotten that morning but my pants.

What's peculiar about this nocturnal horror is that it's a common one, nearly universal. However, the dream is not about physical nudity; it symbolizes the fear that a moment may come when all our secrets, even those from our teenage years, are laid bare for all to see. *Pun intended!* Much like I did in my nightmare, the woman in our story was forced to stand in full view, bearing the heavy burden of shame. Her shame serves as a profound symbol, speaking volumes to us even today.

In some sense, isn't that what we all fear—exposure?

What if they knew what I had been thinking?

What if they saw my internet browser history or read my text messages?

What if they knew what I had done?

What if they knew what had been done to me?

We often deceive ourselves, believing that we're safe as long as our secrets remain hidden. This sense of security is merely an illusion, though, for in hiding we become enslaved to those secrets. The longer we allow sin to remain concealed, the tighter and more unyielding its grip becomes on our souls. This inevitably leads to a pressing and uncomfortable question: If we find ourselves living with deep, dark secret sins, whom can we confide in? Unfortunately, the church has not always done a commendable job of addressing the painful secrets that people bear. Some churchgoers seem to view their so-called ministry as the mission to catch individuals in their wrongdoing just so they can label, define, and stigmatize them.

The story of this woman caught *flagrante delicto* prompts an intriguing question: Where was the man? If the woman was caught in the act, the man must have been present too. Why was it only she bore the shame before the crowd? Christine Caine's insight seems fitting here; she writes, "One could argue that the woman was brought for judgment because of her sin, but that would only be partly true. If justice had been the real goal, then the man would have been charged as well. No, this woman was guilty of the crime of being a *woman* caught in adultery."[7] The passage leads us to reflect on deeper biases and unequal applications of justice and how we find it easier to label the powerless. Why does it seem that the woman is always subjected to blame, shame, and punishment?

Even more, something is perplexing about this notion of being caught in the act of adultery. It suggests a deliberate intention behind the actions of the religious leaders who stumbled upon this scene. How does an entire group of religious leaders chance upon an act of adultery? It appears that they were already aware of her wrongdoing and awaited an opportunity to expose her. Their intent was not to offer assistance or support but rather to witness her pay for her sins. The word *caught* carries a deliberate weight. It implies they were aware of her transgressions and sought an occasion to see her falter, all to justify their moral superiority.

If we are honest, isn't this why the world holds contempt for religious people and their institutions? It stems from the perception that they, the religious, are constantly seeking someone to shame. God's law, intended to be good and holy, reflecting our shortcomings, is all too frequently weaponized to cultivate a sense of moral superiority. This twisted use of the law can lead to the belief that if my sins are viewed as less severe than yours, then I can somehow feel superior or more righteous. Such a distortion not only undermines the true purpose of divine law but also creates divisions and resentment within communities.

The challenge we face is not in recognizing and addressing sin but rather in the manner we engage with it. There is value in intervening in a loved one's life to gently call out sinful behavior that may be leading to their destruction, but the line between compassionate conversation and outright condemnation is easily crossed. Jesus' ministry stood as a testament to the former, but the religious leaders in this story were deeply entrenched in the latter—they were the Pharisees, after all.[8] Make no mistake, sin is such a serious matter, it necessitated Christ's sacrifice. To trivialize sin is to reduce the gravity of that sacrifice, but the movement of the gospel is toward grace, not judgment.[9] To make matters worse, these religious leaders brought this woman to the temple to condemn her. Which brings me to an important question: Why do we keep bringing people to church just to condemn them? Isn't it bewildering how some religious people attempt to shame others into salvation? Who came up with this bizarre plan for evangelism? No one surrenders to Jesus through forced conversion. No one enters the kingdom of God on the basis of guilt and condemnation. While fear of judgment may temporarily lead some to profess belief in Jesus, it cannot sustain a genuine and enduring life of devotion. Transformation takes place only when we recognize our sin in the context of God's grace, becoming willing to abandon our transgressions and follow the Savior.[10] We may communicate the most compelling message in the universe, the gospel, with an angry and judgmental attitude, and it will do nothing to bring about the transformation of hearts. It is not the fear of judgment but the kindness and compassion of God that leads us to repentance. The gentleness of grace opens hearts and minds to true and lasting change. And only when we share the message of grace in the spirit of grace will other people become willing to receive the transformative power of grace.

Reflecting on the story of the adulterous woman is probably as discomforting for you as it is for me. The intensity of the moment is lost on none of us. Picture the scene: enraged men, a terrified woman, a congregation bearing witness to her humiliation, and a call for death by stoning. The air was thick with fear and loathing, and the question on everyone's mind was, "What will Jesus do?"

That defining moment transcends time, for the question "What will Jesus do?" echoes in our lives today. We all carry the weight of carefully guarded secrets, internal labels, and past deeds that continually haunt us. Even if we've moved on from the shameful behavior, the residue often clings to our souls. The woman in the story faced the public pronouncement of her worst fears, the labels she might have internalized:

Home wrecker.

Adulteress.

Whore.

Shame emerges as an integral character in this account, and it prompts us to consider how Jesus' response might guide our attitudes toward ourselves and others. This account challenges us to wrestle with a fundamental question: Why is shaming others a part of human behavior? Bestselling author and therapist Brené Brown provides a profound insight: "After studying vulnerability, shame, and authenticity for the past decade, here's what I've learned. A deep sense of love and belonging is an irreducible need of all people. We are biologically, cognitively, physically, and spiritually wired to love, to be loved, and to belong. When those needs are not met, we don't function as we were meant to. We break. We fall apart. We numb. We ache. We hurt others."[11] On some level, we shame others because we ourselves are burdened with shame. Shame perpetuates shame. Just as shame might have been an intrinsic part of the Samaritan woman's identity, it is similarly ingrained in many of us. It's woven into the fabric of our culture, and, unfortunately, sometimes even the church. Our society operates within a framework of shame and honor, where individual worth hinges on adherence to certain values or codes of conduct. In the church, this can intertwine with a religious holiness code, emphasizing specific values and appearances. This focus can overshadow the transformation that is at the heart of our faith, leading to a misunderstanding of purity. The emphasis on external conformity can eclipse the internal formation that is central to biblical spirituality, making appearance more vital than the authenticity of one's spiritual journey.

Shame has no redemptive value; it is corrosive, eroding away the life of the soul. So why do we allow it to live in the dark hallways of our memories? Why do we allow it to break into the light of day with phrases like "shame on you"? The persistence of shame reveals our need for healing—from the lies sown by our adversary, from the wounds of our past, and from debilitating mindsets that never really served us.[12] We must embrace a fresh perspective that guides us toward better living, not through the crippling force of shame but by recognizing and accepting our true selves in light of what Jesus has done for us.

The image of the woman standing before the religious leaders draped in shame haunts me. In it I see the reflection of an entire generation awaiting the church's response to their own failings. This sober picture requires us to confront crucial questions that will shape both our work and our witness for a generation to come. Will we pursue our calling to be a spiritual hospital, or will we yield to the religious tribunal that governs modern evangelicalism? Where do our true priorities lie—in guarding our reputations or in a commitment to guide our generation toward salvation? Our responses to these questions will not only reveal our capacity for Christlike compassion but also test our genuineness in loving others.

John, the gospel writer, doesn't tell us what Jesus wrote in the dirt that day as he rejected the Pharisees' demands for retribution and judgment. Intriguingly, the Bible depicts

God writing on two other occasions: when he descended from heaven to inscribe the Ten Commandments with his finger on stone tablets, and when he delivered a message of judgment on the wall in Babylon. One could speculate that Jesus might have written those same Ten Commandments in the dirt. Though these religious leaders strived to follow all 613 Jewish laws, deep within, they likely knew they had failed to uphold at least one of these commandments, if not more, in their hearts.

The story concludes with the accusers dropping their rocks and slinking back into the crowd that had gathered to watch the spectacle. At that moment, Jesus straightened himself and addressed the woman directly, granting her the dignity unjustly denied by her accusers. He inquired about the whereabouts of her condemners. "Has no one condemned you?"

"No one, sir," she responded.

Then the only one who possessed the authority to condemn her, the sinless one capable of casting the first stone, declared, "Then neither do I condemn you." In this simple yet profound declaration, Jesus not only absolved the woman but also offered a powerful lesson in mercy and grace, transcending the law with love. That day, condemnation was the only thing condemned; shame the only thing put to death. *He did not come to condemn us; he came to rescue us from sin and shame.*[13]

Jesus removed the label, wiped the residue clean, and liberated the woman from her shameful past. Like he did with the woman at the well, he sent her on her way free from condemnation and without even trying to unwind the messiness of her life. He simply encouraged her to "go now and leave your life of sin," to live in the wonder of his grace.[14] Jesus shows us that being labeled is not the same as being defined. Though we may be labeled, he alone defines our worth and value.

One lesser known fact about the woman caught in adultery is the ambiguity surrounding her narrative. While the story is widely accepted, its placement in the Bible is inconsistent across various manuscripts, leading some scholars to debate its originality in John's gospel. The story is absent from many early Greek manuscripts of the Gospel of John, appearing in different locations within different versions of the text. Despite this debate, the account's profound message of grace and forgiveness is consistent with Jesus' behavior and thus has given it enduring relevance down through the ages.

The point of these encounters throughout the Gospels is to give us some insight into God's boundless grace and mercy—his love and kindness in Jesus—but also to show us the kind of behavior expected of all who follow him. We all find ourselves within these stories, whether as the woman facing the gravity of her sins and desperately yearning for forgiveness, the religious leaders committed to her condemnation, the silent onlookers in the crowd, or perhaps even the man who abandoned her in shame. The point is that we should mirror Jesus, embodying his kindness, grace, truthfulness, and forgiveness.

The striking contrast in this story lies in how the Pharisees treated this woman versus the way our Savior embraced her. He approached her, as well as every other person in the Gospels—whether they were "the lost sheep of Israel" or pagan idolaters—with an open heart and unconditional acceptance.[15] His love was demonstrated not by minimizing sin but by maximizing grace. It is essential to remember that Jesus did not ignore or trivialize the woman's sin; instead, he recognized her transgressions, addressing them with compassion and discretion. His actions demonstrated that judgment belongs solely in the hands of God, not those who would use it to exert control or exact punishment.

A few chapters later in the story, Jesus stood before the same religious leaders, accepting judgment not for his sins but for the sins of all humanity. He took our blame and shame in being crucified, enduring a humiliating and painful death. His death was not a tragic end to a beautiful life but a transformative act of love. By accepting our guilt and absorbing our shame, Jesus freed us from condemnation and erased the labels that once defined and confined us. Through his sacrifice, he offered redemption and grace, replacing judgment with mercy and inviting us into a new relationship characterized by forgiveness and acceptance.[16]

Love needs no labels.

chapter 5

truth and tone

the art of compassionate conversations

"Sir," the woman said, "you have nothing to draw with and the well is deep. Where can you get this living water? Are you greater than our father Jacob, who gave us the well and drank from it himself, as did also his sons and his livestock?" Jesus answered, "Everyone who drinks this water will be thirsty again, but whoever drinks the water I give them will never thirst. Indeed, the water I give them will become in them a spring of water welling up to eternal life." The woman said to him, "Sir, give me this water so that I won't get thirsty and have to keep coming here to draw water."

—John 4:11–15

A few years ago, I visited an audiologist to have my hearing tested. Unfortunately, my hearing seems to be diminishing, and for some odd reason, it correlates to the frequency my wife speaks on. She playfully refers to it as "selective hearing"—at least I think that's what she said. After a consultation, the doctor led me into an isolation booth and fitted me with a clunky headset. To my surprise, my hearing was deemed relatively good, dashing my hopes of attributing my listening lapses to a medical condition.

I did discover, however, that because of an auditory processing disorder there are some frequencies that I can't hear anymore. Apparently, as we age, we lose the ability to hear certain high-frequency sounds, especially in loud environments like restaurants, discos, and church services. Okay, I made the disco part up to avoid dancing, but I'm not giving up food or Jesus. Sadly, I don't hear conversations well when there is a lot of background noise, which is a problem, since I spend a lot of time in loud rooms with loads of background noise.

Sometimes it feels like our whole culture is going through an auditory processing disorder and we're losing our ability to hear one another.

Life is loud.

The world is a cacophony of sound, a screeching symphony of noise, where quiet stillness is a precious gift, a rarity that dwindles with each passing day. Gordon Hempton, an acoustic ecologist, mourns the loss of silence, naming it one of the "endangered species" of our modern age.[1] Perhaps it is the turmoil within our own hearts that perpetuates the absence of serenity in the world around us.

When was the last time you found solace in the stillness, contemplating the state of your community, and pondered ways to serve it with grace?

When was the last time you tuned in to the lamentations of those around you and, instead of offering hasty solutions, simply lent an ear and a heart to heal?

When was the last time you listened to the whispers of your neighbors' hearts yearning to be seen, valued, loved?

There are so many raised voices and loud noises clamoring for our attention. I can't remember a time when everyone was screaming at the same decibel level. From politics to products, everyone has their cause, and they are eager to shape our consciousness. I can't imagine what the world will feel like in the future if we keep shouting at one another across tables and on social-media platforms and in forums of every kind.

Amid the cacophony of life, the fight for dominance never ceases. Each technological marvel further intensifies the voices that compete for our attention. Although I embrace the positive potential of technology, I cannot ignore its potential to consume us if we're not vigilant. It has already opened new avenues for spreading hope, yet the path it takes must be carefully monitored to ensure it serves our purposes, not the other way around.

Sometimes the loudest noise isn't around us, it's *in* us.

Do you find your thoughts racing more these days? Do you struggle to quiet your mind? Do you talk out loud to yourself in a desperate attempt to sort through the competing ideas in your head? *Yeah, me neither.* I think that the noise in us is the loudest because we hear it in our own voice. The negative self-talk in our heads is worse than any troll on Twitter.

All of this noise makes it really hard for us to hear ourselves, let alone each other. Deep conversations require the willingness to abide in quiet moments no matter how uncomfortable they make us. Sitting in silence with another person is scary. What if we don't know how to respond? What if the conversation gets heated? What if they say something offensive?

It's easier and so very tempting to jump in with answers, responses, and assumptions when all we really need to do is listen.

The Ministry of Listening

Within the opening verses of her story, the Samaritan woman delivers four lines of dialogue while Jesus responds with only two brief sentences. Her words seem to convey a sense of incredulousness as she questions whether Jesus is greater than Jacob. Instead of becoming defensive or agitated, he remains attentive, curious, genuinely hearing and addressing the underlying pain behind her questions. Perhaps there is something significant for us to glean from this exchange.

The art of listening is an essential skill for every Christian. Approaching others with a willingness to listen, free from judgment or interruption, holds great power in cultivating trust and fostering genuine relationships. Conversely, refusal to listen often leads to assumptions about one another, which become barriers that hinder our witness. When people sense judgment and condemnation, their defenses rise swiftly. But when they feel heard and understood, they find a sense of safety, enabling them to share their stories.

Deep listening does not mean we have to agree with what

is being said, but we must embrace the idea that human connections are more important than conversational outcomes. Something of value may be said that we can learn from.

Throughout their conversation, the Samaritan woman progressively feels safer in the presence of Jesus, allowing her to gradually open up to him. She became receptive to his words as she sensed that her voice was being heard. Jesus' ability to listen attentively amplified her curiosity and receptivity to his message.

Our listening suffers when our curiosity is contained.

Engaging in a ministry of listening surpasses merely leaving gaps in the conversation for others to interject their thoughts. We have all experienced situations where someone remained quiet, yet we knew they were not fully present or attuned to what we were saying. Instead, genuine listening entails offering our undivided attention to the person before us. When we wholeheartedly invest ourselves in a conversation, it influences our tone and manner of responding. We become more intentional about filling silences and more measured in our replies. This profound human connection paves the way for deeper and more compassionate communication.

A Visit to the Vatican

My wife and I recently met with Pope Francis at his papal quarters in the Vatican. We were invited to join him along with a small group of Pentecostal pastors, denominational leaders, and Roman Catholic priests for an evening of dialogue, prayer, and reflection on the importance of unity. To my surprise, after making his way around the small circle to warmly welcome each of us, Pope Francis sat quietly listening to our group for almost an hour before speaking. As a strong advocate for "listening with the ear of the heart" as an aid in healing the wounds of the soul, the pontiff practices what he preaches. He proposed that we each "embrace the apostolate of the ear," meaning that we accept the mission to listen before speaking.[2] This has aided him greatly in avoiding the natural tendency of many leaders to categorize, label, and dismiss people we might otherwise disagree with.

Listening is an expression of love, reflecting our willingness to care, understand, and value others.

Pope Francis's call to use listening as an act of healing brings to mind the courage of Dietrich Bonhoeffer. If there was ever a person who could justify employing a harsh tone when conveying the truth, it would be Bonhoeffer. A German theologian and pastor, he opposed the Nazi regime during the 1930s and '40s, a period marked by the rise of totalitarianism and escalating violence against the Jewish people and marginalized communities. The urgency of these times, as the world grappled with unprecedented political upheaval and moral decay, might have justified a more vehement condemnation of the evils of his day. Yet Bonhoeffer chose not to. Instead, he took great care to guide the church in maintaining a delicate balance between truth and tone, recognizing the importance of both in his ministry.

According to Bonhoeffer, "Christians have forgotten that the ministry of listening has been committed to them by him who is himself the great listener and whose work they should share. We should listen with the ears of God that we may speak the Word of God."[3]

We are called to listen to people as an act of dignity, respect, and honor. Before rushing to judgment, forming uninformed opinions, presuming we know the content and intent of their hearts, and assuming we know why they do what they do, we owe one another the compassionate service of listening. So much of what we assume to know about one another could be radically changed by a willingness to listen.

Listening is a profound act of love, signifying attentiveness and consideration to another's thoughts and emotions. When we listen, we bestow our undivided attention, affirming their presence and worth. This act can make the other person feel seen, heard, and respected. It shows our concern for their views and displays interest in their unique perspectives. It sends the message that we value their experiences—their joys and sorrows, hopes and longings, and fears.

Effective listening requires not only hearing the words being spoken but also understanding the underlying emotions and intentions. It means being present in the moment and not just waiting for our turn to speak. It also means being able to put ourselves in the other person's shoes and see things from their perspective.

Consider Jesus' conversation with the Samaritan woman; it radically transformed her life and had a profound impact on her community. For most of us, a single conversation isn't sufficient to transform someone's perspective. Yet it harbors the potential for something immensely significant: another conversation. One compassionate conversation may not change anything, but a dozen conversations over the course of years have the potential to change everything. Consistent listening, across months and years, creates a safe space, opens hearts, lowers barriers, and dispels the fear of rejection. It encourages others to share their deepest fears and greatest desires.

The ministry of listening is an essential aspect of embodying the love of Jesus and extending grace to those we encounter.

Master Listener

Jesus was a master listener. He could achieve in a single conversation what it takes many of us years to accomplish. We often study his powerful sermons and creative parables but overlook how he engaged people with questions, silence, and strategic pauses. He desired to hear from the people around him. His wisdom was on display in all forms of communication as he engaged people in every way but one—he rarely answered questions directly. Of the 113 questions asked of him in the Gospels, he answered only three of them directly.

Why do we feel compelled to answer every question we are asked about our faith, even when we lack clear and definitive answers? And even if we have clear answers, is it wise to just blurt out the answers without discerning the heart behind the question? In my years of serving as a pastor, I've discovered that the question being asked is rarely the question being asked. In other words, the question usually reflects a deeper issue. Discerning this underlying issue and addressing it, rather than focusing solely on the surface question, echoes the approach Jesus consistently adopted throughout the Gospels.

My parents instilled in me the value of answering questions directly, a lesson that was further reinforced throughout a lifetime of education in the Western world. This directness was portrayed as a sign of respect, acknowledgement, or a willingness to be helpful. (This is not the same in the Near East or the Far East.) Yet as much as I value them, direct answers aren't always the most insightful ones. What if Jesus' approach reflected a wisdom greater than our own? Frequently, he would respond to questions by posing one in return or steering the conversation in an unexpected direction. Secure in his identity and mission, he cared less about appearing omniscient and more about assisting the one questioning in the discovery of something more important than an immediate answer—an invitation to a deeper discovery. If theology was the old apologetic, relational engagement is the new apologetic. More than that, love itself is the ultimate apologetic.

Jesus listened closely to the woman at the well, and his willingness to engage her in a dialogue drew her deeper into his innermost thoughts. Notably, this conversation between Jesus and the Samaritan woman is the longest recorded discussion between Jesus and anyone else in the Gospels. John devotes nineteen verses to the documented part of their exchange. I find this fascinating, knowing that Jesus is on record in the Gospels with more than forty conversations ranging from a few words to a few paragraphs. Sometimes, Jesus said only one quick sentence to a person, like to Jairus's daughter: "Little girl . . . get up!"[4] Yet when it came to the woman at the well, Jesus settled in for his most lengthy conversation.

Why does Jesus take so much time to engage this particular woman in a conversation?

I think it's because of what she represented.

The Samaritan woman embodied the most provocative issues of her times and, interestingly, of ours—the agency of women, power dynamics, racial oppression, sexual identity, religious division, and the role of borders, beliefs, and customs. I'm just old enough to remember when polite conversations didn't include two of those things: politics and religion. In one exchange, Jesus covered every controversial subject that has been argued around dinner tables for the past few decades.

And he engaged her in a way that didn't alienate her; instead, it intrigued her.

Jesus made it a point to listen to someone vastly different from himself with views vastly different from his own. And he didn't sermonize her issue or respond with his set of talking points. Instead, he actually listened. When was the last time you saw that level of kind attention in a conversation between two people of opposing views? Unfortunately, it's becoming rarer and rarer.

Instead of listening out of love and with a desire to learn from someone, we usually listen to respond and, in some cases, retaliate. This kind of selective listening causes us to speak past one another. If we don't listen well, we won't communicate well. In the absence of true listening, we spit out our opinions and attempt to make our cases without exchanging any new information or insight. I've seen many well-intentioned but woefully unprepared Christians attempt to engage others outside our faith with little more than a few bullet points pulled from some conservative media source. They enter the conversation with a template of what they want to communicate, then lay that template on top of whatever the other person is saying.

This prevents them from genuinely connecting with people, because they're thoughtlessly prescribing predetermined solutions instead of listening and empathizing.

Sometimes the most important ministry we can offer is to sit with people who are hurting, give them our full attention, and commit to listening to their stories without interjecting our judgments or explanations.

That kind of listening fosters connection and deepens understanding. Yet far too often we choose the path of more words and less understanding. We turn up the volume on our arguments and refuse to lower it to let anyone else into the conversation. So the noise gets louder and louder and our words get harsher and harsher.

Age of Outrage

In an era characterized by a constant barrage of divisive and inflammatory discourse, it is increasingly important for people to engage in the practice of "active listening" as a means of bridging the divide between different perspectives and promoting civil discourse. This need is born from the cultural phenomenon of "outrage porn," a term coined by Tim Kreider in his book *I Wrote This Book because I Love You*. He asserts that individuals are increasingly indulging in content that evokes outrage and anger, in a bid to affirm their beliefs and feel a false sense of ethical superiority. Outrage, Kreider suggests, is a double-edged sword that initially feels gratifying but gradually corrodes one's being. In a *New York Times* essay, he says, "Outrage is like a lot of other things that feel good but over time devour us from the inside out."[5]

The proliferation of outrage is self-perpetuating, as more engagement leads to more content and a higher tolerance for outrage. Social-media algorithms exacerbate this problem, as they prioritize content that elicits maximum engagement, such as likes, shares, and comments. This not only intensifies the cycle of outrage but also encourages cancel culture and makes people more likely to believe in conspiracy theories and fall for misinformation.

The manifestation of outrage in our current national discourse is marked by a steady increase in hostility and volume, and an erosion of decorum and grace. Public debates are increasingly devoid of civility, and inflammatory statements entrench people even deeper in their ideologies. In this context, the ministry of listening becomes critical, offering a path to restoring respect, decency, and understanding.

In the orchestra of outrage, the solo of serenity resonates.

If the church is serious about following the example of the master listener, then we have our work cut out for us. As theologian Henri Nouwen explains:

> To listen is very hard, because it asks of us so much interior stability that we no longer need to prove ourselves by speeches, arguments, statements, or declarations. True listeners no longer have an inner need to make their presence known. . . . Listening is much more than allowing another to talk while waiting for a chance to respond. Listening is paying full attention to others and welcoming them into our very beings. . . . Listening is a form of spiritual hospitality by which you invite strangers to become friends, to get

to know their inner selves more fully, and even to dare to be silent with you.[6]

Truth in Love

If you have been involved in any conversation about the relationship between church and culture during the past few years, you have heard the debate over the importance of speaking the truth in love. Few people would disagree with that premise; it is our responsibility to communicate both grace and truth to a society that lacks an understanding of either. The challenge lies in how to effectively convey these values.

According to Rick Warren, this has become a battle because "our culture has accepted two huge lies: the first is that if you disagree with someone's lifestyle, you must fear or hate them. The second is that to love someone means you agree with everything they believe or do. Both are nonsense. You don't have to compromise convictions to be compassionate."[7] If you believe those lies, then speaking truth becomes a shouting match and love can feel like compromise.

Love and truth are inherently interwoven, deeply connected at their very essence. As the epitome of love, God encompasses all truth within himself. Love is a selfless force that prioritizes the well-being of others, demonstrated through acts of kindness, forgiveness, and understanding. It is an expression of care and empathy. Truth, on the other hand, underlies our belief system, our worldview, our view of others, and responsibility for their well-being. The grounding of truth should be in the reality of Jesus as revealed in the Scriptures, reflecting the wisdom embodied in his life and teachings.

The challenge of speaking the truth in love is both a profound cultural and spiritual undertaking, demanding a delicate equilibrium between honesty, compassion, authenticity, empathy, and understanding. It is a balance that calls for spiritual maturity, self-control, humility, and a readiness to admit mistakes. In a time when political correctness often eclipses truth and the avoidance of offense can obstruct honest dialogue, Jesus' followers must navigate this balance with grace and precision. Truth and tone form an inseparable partnership in our witness to the world.

As acclaimed author and pastor Mark Batterson aptly noted, "Grace without truth is weak sauce; truth without grace is hot sauce; but grace and truth are our secret sauce."[8] Serving as the lead pastor of National Community Church in Washington, DC—a unique congregation situated on Capitol Hill—Mark has skillfully navigated this delicate balance for more than two decades. His leadership has fostered a church community that embraces individuals on both sides of the political aisle.

Imagine grace and truth as two ends of a tightly stretched rubber band. That's a picture of our conversations regarding the most provocative topics of our times. The tension is uncomfortable, and we fight the urge to yield the resistance on one side or the other. Yet maintaining this tension, as exhausting as it may be, is essential to sharing our faith. We are called to an equal commitment to gracious dialogue and unwavering biblical truth. Love sustains us in this space, empowering us to speak truth from a place of genuine concern and compassion.

Love holds the tension between grace and truth.

Our motivation to speak the truth must stem from a heartfelt longing to assist others as they navigate the turbulent waters of confusion and misinformation. Love compels us to draw near enough to whisper truth to them when shouting from a distance might be easier. God's wisdom often contradicts societal norms, and truth may seem confrontational even when shared with love. However, this should not dissuade us from the demanding but sacred duty of conveying truth with affection and empathy. We are called to be truth-tellers and burden-bearers, representing Jesus to the world in both word and deed. The truth is of utmost importance, and so is the manner in which we communicate it. In the words of Warren Wiersbe, "Truth without love is brutality, and love without truth is hypocrisy."[9] Every truth holds profound significance, yet not every truth demands immediate disclosure. Though he was the embodiment of truth, Jesus, in his infinite wisdom, exercised discretion, refraining from revealing the entirety of truth in a single moment. The beauty of God's grace is that he is careful about imposing truth on us without first cultivating our hearts. Instead, he begins an intimate connection with us, tenderly revealing truth as we are ready to receive it. In much the same way, he graciously provides us with the gift of time, allowing us to truly know him and cultivate unwavering trust along the journey. He calls us to emulate this patient and loving approach as we interact with others, expressing truth saturated with grace and discretion. Truth should be used not as a weapon for conformity but as a means for liberation. It is not about compelling compliance but about setting hearts free. While truth can *feel* confining, it unshackles us, revealing our true selves and deepest desires and liberating us from any constraints that might diminish, dehumanize, or bind us.

Often, however, we compromise God's truth in favor of our tribal teachings. Worse, we equate our values with God's truth, which produces confusion in the hearts and minds of the people we are trying to reach. When we assume that our tribe possesses the entirety of truth, we are less likely to listen to others with differing perspectives.

Living in an age of social media has magnified this disproportionately. Social-media algorithms curate what we're exposed to and create echo chambers—comfortable feedback loops of information from voices we agree with, all confirming our opinions. An echo chamber reinforces a group's shared beliefs, to the exclusion of opposing ideas. Information and ideas are selectively presented or distorted to align with the group's preconceived notions. This can isolate us from different views and potentially lead to extremism in our beliefs, stifling critical thinking and reinforcing misinformation.

The deeper we venture into the echo chamber, the less inclined we are to value people with differing opinions. We start associating comfort with truth and disagreement with falsehood, turning our quest for truth into a search for even more voices confirming the echo.

Tyler McKenzie offers this litmus test to determine whether you've wandered into an echo chamber without realizing it: "If the truth stops offending you, you should be very concerned. God's kingdom and his Word transcend all of our artificial political parties, religious sects, cultural worldviews, and ideological tribes. They affirm the goodness in each but also judge the brokenness. If we truly serve a transcendent God, we should be suspicious if he ever starts looking too American, too white, too progressive, too Republican, too whatever."[10] We should expect to be challenged by the truth and be willing to embrace the joy and agony of personal transformation.

Few people in the modern age have demonstrated this blend of veracity and civility better than Martin Luther King Jr. During some of the most heated and divisive moments in modern history, Dr. King modeled the art of gracious speech while also defying those who opposed the civil rights of all people. He advocated for civil disobedience and rallied his supporters to take a stand against racial injustice, systemic poverty, and the Vietnam conflict. But his approach to civil disobedience was practiced within the framework of nonviolence. He spoke truth to power without eviscerating his opponents. And he eschewed ad hominem attacks on others.

When the Supreme Court ordered Montgomery's buses to be desegregated, in December 1956, the Montgomery Improvement Association held two meetings to prepare for when protesters would return to the buses. Although their victory was already secured, Dr. King knew the ultimate battle would continue and his supporters had to maintain their apologetic of love. He wrote to encourage them to show courtesy and humility, to absorb evil and not retaliate, to lead with love and goodwill, and to be wise enough to turn an enemy into a friend. He concluded, "For the first few days try to get on the bus with a friend in whose nonviolence you have confidence. You can uphold one another by a glance or a prayer."[11]

Dr. King's model for noncombative resistance originates in Jesus' practices, although he saw it practiced in other faiths as well. Whether in victory or defeat, Dr. King maintained a focus on loving his enemies in the hope that they would embrace the truth. The goal wasn't to win the battle and humiliate his opponents. The goal was to see the oppressors change their behavior and participate with them in the work of being the beloved community.

While laws are powerful and the state can compel people into compliance, only the love of Jesus can make a person want to change.

Dr. King recognized this. Many activists today do not. I love the activist spirit of the emerging generation, but I do not love the spirit in which some of them are active. Many have chosen to speak their truth in anger, fear, and even hatred. Setting fire to institutions without regard for those who exist within them is not helpful. The chants to "burn it all down" feel nothing to me like the spirit of Jesus, who prophesied with tears on his cheeks that the temple would be destroyed (only to be replaced with something better).[12] The church must resist this lower form of activism that does nothing to improve the conditions of our communities. Christians must have a markedly different tone from that of the world around us.

Compassionate Conversations

Throughout his ministry, Jesus showed us the art of compassionate conversation. He spoke the truth as a loving observation and never used it as a destructive weapon. This is a beautiful example of practicing radical kindness toward people unlike us.

Jesus desired to connect with people, and he listened not just to their words but also to their deeper needs. But he didn't force himself on people—he was the master of the segue, on the lookout for any opening that invited him deeper in. Jesus was far more than a surface-level communicator; he was a profound connector. His desire to connect with people went beyond mere words and reached into the depths of their hearts, uncovering hidden needs and unspoken desires. Yet his approach was never intrusive or forceful. He was the master of the segue, seamlessly transitioning into deeper matters, always on the lookout for an opening that invited him farther into a person's life. His interactions were marked by a delicate balance of wisdom and tact, showing that true communication is not just about speaking but about understanding, responding, and bridging the gap between minds and hearts.

We see this on display when the woman at the well asked about water. Jesus knew that what she really needed was living water. So he segued into a much deeper conversation. It's as though Jesus looked at each person and thought, "How can I help her?" "Does he need to know how much God loves him?" "Will there be an opening to tell her that?" I wonder what it would be like if we looked at people this way.

Sadly, a lot of Christian discourse today fails to include the compassion and kindness that Jesus modeled for us. We fail to acknowledge and appreciate the *co-* in communication. The prefix *co-* means "with" or "together jointly." Sharing with each other like partners. Think of the words *collaborate*, *cooperate*, or *coworker*. Communication should be a two-way partnership in which we participate back and forth. Those two letters speak to the value, importance, and benefit of the other, yet far too often when we try to communicate the love and truth of the gospel, we are doing so not *with* the other but *to* or *against* the other. What does it say to the world when we weaponize our faith and use it to fight those who disagree with us?

Thankfully, there is another way. There is a growing movement within the church that asserts that our posture in communicating the gospel matters as much as our position. Winsome communication is a corrective movement away from the selfish insistence that as long as we can defend the doctrine of our stance, our tone and timing don't matter. Winsome communication is focused not on winning an argument but rather on lovingly engaging the other person. We bring into the conversation the things we know, along with a desire to know the other more.

Are we trying to win arguments or win people to Jesus?

If we are trying to win arguments, we will face off against people as if they were opponents in a debate. Then when we feel like we've won the discussion by sharing enough truth, we can proudly walk away and pat ourselves on the back for a job well done.

But as Tomáš Halík, Czech philosopher and priest, says, "Truth *happens* in the course of dialogue."[13] In medieval times, debates did not have winners or losers, because everyone was seeking the truth together. Arguments were meant to deepen friendship in a common quest for knowledge. When knowledge was uncovered, it was a source of great celebration, because what each truth seeker was looking for individually was now available to be shared, experienced, and enjoyed by both.

If we are trying to win people to Jesus, then grace must be extended before truth can be heard—really heard. Extending grace is a way of welcoming people in. Theologian Miroslav

Volf reminds us that Jesus "was no prophet of 'inclusion,' for whom the chief virtue was acceptance and the cardinal vice intolerance. Instead, he was a bringer of 'grace,' who not only scandalously included 'anyone' in the fellowship of 'open commensality' but also made the 'intolerant' demand of repentance and the 'condescending' offer of forgiveness."[14] This concept resonates deeply with me because it challenges the common accusation that those who love and include the other are merely succumbing to the tide of public opinion or diluting biblical values to gain acceptance in the culture. There may be some who do that, but they are in the minority. In truth, the path of grace is not one of convenience or complacency. It's infinitely more demanding and requires a strength of character to take grace to those in need, especially when you are accused of having ulterior motives. Following the way of Jesus in this regard is not just a reflection of acceptance, it's an embodiment of a profound, transformative love that reaches out to heal and uplift.

Jesus had a remarkable ability to include people in his world. Where others drew lines, he drew circles. Where others erected barriers, he built bridges. Where others emphasized differences, he stressed the things his followers had in common with him and each other. No one was excluded from the inclusive nature of his grace. In his way of embracing all, Jesus was modeling the kind of behavior he expected his followers to embrace.

Salvation is found only in Jesus; therefore, the exclusivity of the gospel is central to the Christian faith. But this exclusive nature did not conflict with Jesus' unparalleled inclusivity. He was the most inclusive individual in Scripture, throwing wide open the door to anyone and everyone willing to trust him for their salvation. Throughout the Gospels, we see the tension of this exclusive-inclusive paradigm expressed in his life, teaching, and ministry. His exclusivity was demonstrated in the calling of his disciples, his teachings on the cost of discipleship, and his requirements to the rich young ruler. His inclusivity was modeled by his interactions with children, women, sinners, and even lepers. In Jesus, the overlooked and rejected find love, hope, and acceptance, showing us a way forward that transcends divisive distinctions and connects us in the shared pursuit of grace.

Love shouldn't be confined to the narrow parameters of agreement or approval. Jesus exemplified a model of love that reaches beyond the state of someone's life, the content of their beliefs, or their attitude toward us. He taught us to love everyone, even our enemies, providing a framework for compassion that defies worldly limitations.

In our polarized world, this concept of love can be hard to grasp. Society often conditions us to see life as a constant battle of us versus them, where every encounter is a competition with winners and losers. But the reality is that fear often fuels this polarization. It's fear that stifles the growth of love and keeps us from truly understanding and embracing the unsurpassable love of God. To truly love as Jesus taught us, we must challenge this fear, dig deep to uncover its roots, and replace it with an expansive and fearless love.

Learning to speak the truth in love requires that we drive out fear, first and foremost. Only then can we engage with others in a way that reflects the profound and inclusive love Jesus modeled for us.[15]

Jesus' conversation with the woman at the well was overflowing with love from beginning to end. Love compelled him to seek her out. Love compelled him to listen. Love compelled him to ask questions, engage mystery, and seek knowledge alongside her. Love compelled him to share the truth in a tone that was both compassionate and kind.

Here's the thing to remember: when we choose to love those who are different from us, we are loving not only them but also Jesus himself.[16] As we navigate the tensions between grace and truth, between our convictions and the call to engage others, let's strive to be agents of transformation in our communities. Together we can challenge stereotypes, build bridges, and cultivate a culture of love, acceptance, and understanding among people who would naturally be opposed toward one another.

chapter 6

the scarlet
letters

navigating guilt, shame,
and acceptance

*The woman said to him, "Sir, give me this
water so that I won't get thirsty and have to
keep coming here to draw water." He told
her, "Go, call your husband and come back."
"I have no husband," she replied. Jesus said
to her, "You are right when you say you have
no husband. The fact is, you have had five
husbands, and the man you now have is not
your husband. What you have just said is
quite true."*

—John 4:15–18

I vaguely recall reading *The Scarlet Letter* in my English Literature class during my sophomore year of high school. I had plenty of things on my mind, and English Lit was not at the top of the list. My primary interests were Jesus, church, ministry, girls, and football—and not necessarily in that order.

I had landed in a football-player development lab entirely by accident when my dad became the pastor of a little church in a nearby town. Seven NFL players have come out of the high school I attended, and in a little town of four thousand people, that was no small accomplishment. Honestly, although I played football, I spent little time on the field. Most of it was on the bench with the other skinny kids, in the huddle supporting our beefy teammates, or in the locker room getting hazed.

There is one thing that was even worse than the locker room, and that was my English Lit class. Here the hazing wasn't from other players; it was from my teacher, who desperately tried to inspire us to love the classics. Sadly, her demeanor triggered the opposite reaction in most of us. She introduced us to *The Catcher in the Rye*, *To Kill a Mockingbird*, *Lord of the Flies*, *Of Mice and Men*, and, of course, *The Scarlet Letter*. She also introduced us to low self-esteem when we failed to meet her impossibly high standards.

Nathaniel Hawthorne wrote *The Scarlet Letter* in 1850. It follows the story of Hester Prynne as she navigates Puritan society in the midseventeenth century. When Hester has a child out of wedlock, she is forced to wear a scarlet *A* to mark her as an adulterer forever. This punishment assures her sin will never be forgotten, and she will never stop paying the price.

Though most people are familiar with *The Scarlet Letter*, few are aware of a short story published by Nathaniel

Hawthorne fourteen years earlier. *The Minister's Black Veil* set the tone for his later masterpiece, and it also concerned hidden sins.

Reverend Hooper is the main character of *The Minister's Black Veil*. He wears a black veil over his face to show how sin damages lives and separates people from one another. The veil symbolizes secret sins that get in the way of our genuine connections despite how hard we try to hide them.

Hawthorne's gloomy thoughts about human behavior haunted me as a sophomore wanting to focus on things other than literature. Decades later, I have some insight into his pre-occupation, but the feeling remains. At the risk of aggravating English Lit teachers everywhere, I would like to modify his titles based on the times in which we live. We live in the age of *The Scarlet Alphabet* and *The Minister's Invisible Veil*.

In our world today, many frame the letters *LGBTQIA+*[1] as scarlet letters, labeling and condemning people who wear them in the loudest and harshest of ways. At the same time, the religious community has witnessed more than our share of hidden sins carefully masked by the people in the pulpits, despite their constant moralizing and sermonizing.

Some of the harshest preachers in recent history have hidden the most egregious sins.

I write that sentence reluctantly because those who have preached law and have fallen hard are a cheap and easy target. Yet it's worth considering: Why do those who condemn others the hardest and in the most arrogant and condescending tones often end up being exposed for some hidden sin in their own lives? Why do people who hammer truth and withhold grace often end up bloodied by the one and most in need of the other?

The Western church has exemplified hypocrisy on issues especially related to sexuality. It is on display when we obsessively point out the sexual proclivities of those on the margins and cover up the sexual sins of people in power. Sadly, this hypocrisy is nothing new; it even reaches back to biblical times.[2]

Perhaps no other person in the Bible has been so highly judged and identified by her sexual history as the Samaritan woman.

I can't remember the first time I heard her story. For that matter, as a PK who attended church three times a week, I can't remember when I heard *any* Bible story for the *first* time. (A PK is a pastor's kid. Yes, we had our own label, and some wore it like a badge of honor.) Even though I can't recall hearing most Bible stories for the *first* time, I have vague impressions of hearing them as a child, particularly the feelings they evoked in me.

Every telling of the Samaritan woman involved words describing her moral state.

Conservative pastors, like my father, used terms like "woman of ill repute," but that's because my dad is big on decorum. Other pastors who were less Victorian would push the envelope and call her a "prostitute" or a "harlot." And I remember one visiting evangelist who broke all the rules and called her a "whore."

On Sunday morning.

In our little, conservative church.

When he shouted the words "She was a whore!" time stood still.

You could have heard a pin drop.

I can remember feeling a combination of shock and, quite honestly, curiosity. *What is a whore and why does everything suddenly feel so weird in this auditorium? Also, why is everyone suddenly so interested in their shoes?*

Why has the church labeled her a prostitute? That descriptor is not found anywhere in the text. Jesus doesn't call her that. So why have some of us?

Understanding the Samaritan Woman

Down through the ages, the Samaritan woman has been stereotypically described as sexually promiscuous, with few exceptions. Often those narratives reflect the complexity of Christian perspectives on women in general at the times in which they were written. The Samaritan woman epitomizes the idea that a minority woman with multiple marriages, a confident demeanor in conversing with men, and a different belief system is suspected of being anything but virtuous. Despite the Scriptures making no such claim about her, the church has rendered its verdict, and as is the case, the judgment has become a label, and we all know how sticky those can be.

The first assault on her character came in the third century when Tertullian of Carthage (155–220) asserted his opinion as fact. Based solely on the description in John's gospel, he declared, "To the Samaritan woman, now during her sixth marriage not only an adulteress but also a prostitute—and yet the Lord displayed who he was to her, which he did not easily do."[3] In one sweeping condemnation, he labeled the woman and diminished the grace of her Savior—*"Which he did not easily do."* Did Tertullian really think that showing grace to this woman was difficult for Jesus? Let me clarify this once and for all. Unequivocally.

Grace comes as effortlessly to Jesus as your next breath will come to you. There is never a moment when showing grace is something he does not easily do. He is always moving *toward* his children with love, eagerly seeking them, prepared to bestow his boundless gift of grace upon each and every one.

The question is this: What are *we* moving toward?

Grace or judgment?

Love or labels?

Acceptance or rejection?

A century after Tertullian's theological blunder, John Chrysostom (347–407) proclaimed the woman's marital history wicked and shameful from his lofty pulpit in Constantinople. But he honored her conversion and subsequent elevation to the highest ministry office. He wrote, "She did apostolic work by announcing the good news to all, calling them to Jesus, and bringing the whole city out to him."[4]

Twelve hundred years later, John Calvin (1509–64) dealt the most severe judgment from his pulpit in Geneva. He described her as a "slut; an unhappy, poor, and common woman; a prostitute undeserving of God's grace."[5]

The trend continues across many evangelical, conservative, and fundamentalist pulpits today. But how accurate is this perception? Was she a promiscuous sinner, a wanton temptress, a femme fatale, or has the church actually missed a better interpretation in its rush to label this woman?

Here are a few things to consider.

She lived two thousand years ago in a world utterly unlike

our own. The culture, customs, and context are as different from ours as the sun's surface is to the ocean's floor.

Combining our lack of understanding of first-century Near Eastern culture with the presumption that we understand the intricacies of the times creates a toxic mixture of illiteracy and ignorance.

Every first-year seminary student comes away with one big idea that sticks with them for the rest of their lives: context matters. They may not remember the finer points of epistemology, ecclesiology, and eschatology. Still, they know that something happened in a time and place far, far away and that something may not be like anything that happens around them daily—even if it is named the same.

That's why we should approach every biblical text with humility and curiosity, even if we've read it a hundred times. Setting aside our preconceived notions will lead to a better understanding of the Samaritan woman's context and the importance of this account in the Gospels. And, even as we read her story with an open heart and mind, we must remember that there is still a lot that we don't know about women's lives in the first century because the records were written in a patriarchal culture where their voices, experiences, and stories were not recorded.

Perhaps no one understands the world of the Samaritan woman quite like Dr. Lynn Cohick. Having delved deep into the cultures of the first-century world, she has generously shared her research with her students and readers for more than two decades. Her scholarly work has laid the foundation for many books and articles, mine among them. But her contributions extend beyond mere academic discourse; she's breathed life into the Samaritan woman's story in a way that resonates with our contemporary hearts and minds.[6]

The Samaritan woman's marital history may appear damning through our modern lens, but viewed through a first-century Near Eastern, Jewish, or Samaritan perspective, it alters dramatically.

In the Samaritan woman's era, societal norms and social circumstances often led girls to marry in their mid to late teens, typically binding them to husbands who were often a decade or more their senior. This cultural practice was shaped by the harsh realities of the time, including high mortality rates stemming from diseases, accidental fatalities, and complications in childbirth. Such conditions often limited the duration of these marriages to an average of around fifteen years. Within this context, the Samaritan woman's experience of multiple marriages can be viewed with a more nuanced understanding, providing insight into the complexities of her life and the societal framework that influenced her journey.[7]

Upon a spouse's death, women found themselves in a vulnerable position, because they inherited nothing from their husbands and were permitted to retain only what they'd brought into the marriage: their possessions and dowry. This scenario brings into sharper relief the Samaritan woman's predicament of potentially losing a spouse and falling into poverty and destitution.

Cultural and religious expectations encouraged widows to remarry to ensure offspring, improve social standing, and secure financial stability. Even the Old Testament mandated that if a man died childless, his brother was to marry the widow, with their firstborn son preserving the deceased's lineage. Therefore, after each loss of a husband, the Samaritan woman likely faced pressure to remarry.

Undeniably, there lies a possibility that the Samaritan woman was a divorcée, not a widow. But when placed against the canvas of societal norms and conditions of her time, this conjecture loses its credibility.

The Samaritan woman was a product of a society deeply rooted in honor and shame. The act of wedding a divorcée, let alone a proven adulteress, carried a weight of shame that few men would embrace. It was also a patriarchal society where anything that made one man reject a woman would also make her unappealing to future husbands. This makes repeated divorces highly unlikely.

Furthermore, according to the law of Moses, a man could choose to divorce his wife, often leaving the woman little say in the matter.[8] Women were considered a husband's most valued possession and, as such, were treated as chattel—often affectionately, but always possessively. It stands to reason that if she was divorced five times, she would have had little say in the matter.[9] As Dr. Lynn Cohick concludes, "It is more likely that her five marriages and current arrangement were the result of unfortunate events that took the lives of several of her husbands."[10]

Is it possible she was cohabiting, coupling, conjugating, or *cuffing* with a man?

Possibly, but let's not rush to judgment.

In Roman society, cohabitation was a common alternative to formal marriage. It's possible that her last partner was a Roman citizen, and she was following the practices of his culture. Or perhaps she was betrothed to the man but not yet married. As we see with Mary and Joseph, there was a betrothal period before the marriage began. This may be what Jesus meant; we don't exactly know. What we do know is that there is absolutely nothing in the text that says that she did anything sinful to be in her current position. Yet we put that scarlet letter on her chest anyway.

Beyond the context of the Samaritan woman's life, there is also some context in this passage that calls into question the label we've put on her. The woman's neighbors expressed no reluctance in believing her testimony about Jesus. She had enough social clout to summon at least some of the people to come meet Jesus, and many of them believed because of her testimony. She may have been an outcast with a scarlet letter, but people trusted her enough to believe what she said. If she were a prostitute or a known adulteress, would they have listened to her and trusted her testimony? Life had dealt the Samaritan woman a harsh hand, multiple times over. Yet she rose above the societal disdain to become a trusted voice. Her story urges us to reconsider our quick judgments of those around us.

Life had not been kind to the Samaritan woman, regardless of her marital history. Even if she had been widowed five times, a situation beyond her control may have created a stain on her character. And based on what we know about her life, she may have been mature, much older than Jesus.

Little Towns, Big Labels

I was born in a small town.

Actually, the town was so small that it didn't have a hospital, so I was born in a nearby town that did have one. Two days after I was born, my parents brought me home to Palmyra, Illinois, and a few days later, the sign at the edge of town had to be changed from 698 to 699. There were plenty of advantages to growing up in a small town, but privacy was not one of them.

Small towns can be great if you live a perfect life, but if you have any history at all, even if you're not to blame, small towns can be the worst.

Even though we don't know the details of the Samaritan woman's history, it's clear that it defined her day-to-day life in a small village. You can *feel* it as you read the story. She was an outsider in her own community, and she lived under the stigma of her past. She didn't have a scarlet letter sewn onto her dress, but she probably understood the sense of isolation and loneliness that plagued Hester Prynne. In small towns, the past casts long shadows. Imagine the Samaritan woman living with whispers and sidelong glances. Do you know anyone carrying a heavy past, perhaps unfairly, in your own community?

But Jesus allowed none of that to influence him. Instead, he treated her with dignity and respect. Although he knew the shame that she bore from the moment they met, he spoke to her with kindness. Jesus never described her complicated and storied past as "sinful," like he did with the woman caught in adultery. The Samaritan woman, shunned and isolated, found dignity and respect in her encounter with Jesus. How are we emulating Jesus in our interactions with those who bear the marks of a stigmatized past?

As we examine her context, the Samaritan woman's story becomes clearer. She had likely experienced traumatic losses and deep pain. And then ostracism and rejection on top of it. As a result, she felt like she didn't belong anywhere. And this was reinforced by the sideways glances and cutting comments of her neighbors.

Who is it in our world who regularly feels the sting of rejection and the judgmental gossip of their neighbors? Who are the stigmatized people we pass by every day? Just as the Samaritan woman came to the well in the heat of the day to avoid the stares, glares, and whispers of the judgmental villagers for reasons beyond our knowledge, we have people in our own world living in the shadows of shame while hiding in plain sight. We all live side by side with modern-day Samaritans— those who bear the brunt of societal judgment. Can we play a part in dissipating the shadows of shame they live in?

How can we see them?

How can we engage them?

How can we alleviate shame instead of reinforcing it?

Our Changing World

Jesus never shied away from identifying and calling out sin. Yet the story of the woman caught in adultery is the only time he directly addressed sexual immorality with an individual. Other times he confronted sins such as hypocrisy, greed, corrupt business practices, uncharitableness, and pretentiousness. Is the church's track record of condemning sin consistent with Jesus' priorities? Do we spend as much time and energy talking about greed, religious hypocrisy, and corrupt business practices as we do about sexual sin? Or have we elevated sexual sin above all else?

In the past five decades, our culture's conversation on sexual identity has changed very quickly. It wasn't that long ago when we witnessed the first publicly gay character on television, which created no small stir. In 1971, *All in the Family* featured a gay character, and the public backlash was intense. Even President Nixon chimed in, equating homosexuals with whores and bashing the network for glorifying either of them. At that point in American culture, most gay people lived in a shadowy world hidden from view and subject to the stereotypes that many heterosexuals harbored against them. Many thought (and still think) they were all promiscuous and predatory, driven by an agenda to remap the landscape of public life, civil marriage, and the education of our children. Over time, as LGBTQIA+ people emerged from the shadows, many heterosexuals began to discover something surprising: not all gay people are the same. In many ways, they are as diverse as the straight community.

I know that idea doesn't play well in conservative circles. And, as someone who believes in a conservative sex ethic and traditional marriage, I realize this may cost me a few credibility points among conservatives. In fact, it may cost me a lot. But there is nothing to be gained by reducing a group of people to a single monolithic stereotype. I've spent considerable time in recent years reexamining my theological beliefs and I still believe homosexuality is inconsistent with God's original design; it is the result of our sinful, fallen state. And yet I see the need to relate to others with kindness and compassion more than ever.

Over the past few decades, I have engaged with a diverse range of individuals, including gay conservatives, theologians, parents, and ministers. These conversations have covered a broad spectrum of perspectives, from those who advocate against premarital sex, same-sex sexual conduct outside of marriage, and all forms of pornography, to those who stand firm against the exploitation of women and children, and injustice in all its manifestations. Among these voices, I have spoken with Christians who identify as being gay and yet have chosen celibacy, viewing their sexual orientation as something to be surrendered in union with Christ's crucifixion. For them, acknowledging their identity is an act of self-awareness and an attempt to live authentically, rather than a description of their sexual behavior. The point I am trying to make is that the LGBTQIA+ community is no more monolithic than any other demographic, yet many Christians view them as if they are all the same.

One scarlet label encompasses them all. The rapidly changing conversations on sexual identity invite us to rethink how we interact with people around us. Just as the Samaritan woman was more than her marital history, people are more than their sexual identities. Can we extend love and compassion rather than condemnation and rejection?

Good Doctrine, Hard Hearts

The faith community has responded to today's shifting social mores in two opposite ways. People at one extreme believe that the biblical teachings on sexuality are restricted to the context in which they were written. They argue that those rules do not apply to modern society because they refer only to a specific time, place, and culture. They claim any biblical exegesis that does not allow for same-sex practices is a bad interpretation of the Scriptures.

People at the other extreme have come out harshly, with loathing and disgust, against the LGBTQIA+ community. In their rush to combat what they see as a clear disregard for, or misuse of, biblical passages, they have ignored an opportunity to listen, love, and show compassion to those who disagree. They've thrown the weight of their energy and outrage into opposing people who embrace a contextual approach to sexuality, instead of building relationships with them.

The tension between these two extremes has caused a lot of pain for everyone involved. I've seen the emotional pain on the faces of parents who are trying to make sense of it all. I've had conversations with young people who left the church after they no longer felt welcome because of their sexual orientation. I've seen pastors forced to choose between their conservative congregations and their desire to minister to everyone in their community. Sadly, the tone of the conversation more than the content of the conversation has damaged our witness to the very community that we're contending over.

After years of seeing Christians engaged in the culture wars and enraged at people with alternative views, the unchurched have come to see us as hateful, homophobic, and hypocritical. Whether you or I personally reflect that or not, that's the witness the church has portrayed to our greater culture—the very people we are called to engage based on God's kindness, compassion, and love. As Russell Moore reminds us, "In some sectors of evangelical America, it seems the only disqualifying character flaw is the failure to hate the right people with the right amount of anger. What is 'power of any kind' if it comes with a loss of moral witness? Nothing."[11]

I think he's right.

Sometimes, as Christians, we can be absolutely right in our convictions, and categorically wrong in how we express them. As in the first century, some preach Christ as a weapon of contention and not as the means of liberation.[12] At some point, those who follow Jesus and seek to represent him faithfully to others must face the truth that despising LGBTQIA+ people *is* a sin. And when it comes to our witness to them, our recent history has created a barrier that's almost impossible to surmount. Ours is a show-and-tell gospel, and the telling part is ineffective when the showing part is absent.

Jesus never despised anyone; instead, he demonstrated unconditional love for those despised by others.

The more I discuss this issue with younger generations, Christian and non-Christian, gay and straight, the more I hear the phrase "clarity is kindness." I think there is a lot to be said about the importance of not offering a bait-and-switch approach to inviting people into our faith communities only for them to find they aren't as welcome as they thought. Pretending to accept everyone just to get them across the threshold of the church before doubling down on our desire to quickly change them is distasteful to everyone involved and may even set back the witness of the church. At the same time, we cannot deceive ourselves into believing that just being clear equates to kindness. I've met a lot of fundamentalists who are very clear in their doctrine but extremely unkind in their presentation of it. We need clarity and kindness.

Let me be clear about one thing: I am not advocating for

a change in how we interpret the Scriptures, I am advocating for a change in how we express them. Although many Christians hold differing views on how to interpret the seven notable passages concerning homosexual behavior, I haven't seen any evidence to convince me that these passages have been interpreted wrongly. I understand the nuance within the text, but I think they've been interpreted accurately. The point I'm making is this: How does it benefit us to have good doctrine if we have hard hearts?[13]

The gospel isn't the basis for who God is opposed to; it is the expression of his desire to reconcile with the whole world. This message of reconciliation should be the beacon guiding all followers of Jesus. Unfortunately, in the Western religious landscape, it often appears that God's people have become better known for their objections and disagreements than for their reflection of this unifying message. This unfortunate perception has overshadowed the gospel's profound message of love and reconciliation, calling for a deep and thoughtful reassessment of how we communicate and live out our faith.

Jesus engaged everyone in his ministry with love and kindness, a practice that caused the religious elite to label him a drunkard and sinner.[14] So why are his followers defined by whom they exclude? How did we earn the label anti-gay, anti-trans, anti-immigrant, and, for that matter, anti-anything? And what does it mean that the biggest backlash comes not from those outside the evangelical world but from the next generation of young people within it? As young people leave the church in droves, they often cite the church's response to the LGBTQIA+ community at the heart of their reluctance to stay. Although Jesus' ministry was defined by love, many in the next generation can see only our hate.

We've lost sight of how we can love and accept others without accepting, affirming, or celebrating their behaviors. Acceptance is not an affirmation; we don't need to fear the two being conflated. Constantly reminding people who pursue alternative lifestyles that "I love you but I don't accept your behavior" isn't helpful if you desire to see them change. Do you constantly say that to your other friends who struggle in other areas, like gossip or pride or financial sin?

The notion of "loving the sinner but hating the sin" may not serve our relationships or our faith in the best way. Even more, it isn't entirely accurate. It's a catchy little aphorism that Christians use to avoid the work of communicating the nuanced position Jesus expressed in the Gospels. When he summed up the Law and prophets in the commandment to love God and love your neighbor, he didn't attach any qualifier to that injunction.[15] Nowhere does he instruct us to "love the sinner, hate the sin," and neither does any other biblical contributor. The closest we come to the phrase is when Jude, commonly thought to be Jesus' younger brother, encourages us to express love and tenderness to sinners while not allowing their sin to defile us.[16] If anything, we should love others unconditionally and monitor the contents of our own hearts carefully. Adam Hamilton takes this idea even farther, suggesting that when Jesus told his followers to love their neighbors, he avoided framing it as "loving the sinner." Hamilton believes that such framing would risk turning the focus onto the sin rather than the person. It could lead to a mindset where one might view the relationship in a condescending manner, thinking, "You are a sinner, but I graciously choose to love you anyway." He argues that this outlook is, perhaps unintentionally, self-righteous and misses the essence of Jesus' message.[17]

As disciples following the way of Jesus, it is far more productive for us to see others as neighbors rather than sinners, keeping in mind that we embody both roles. We, too, are sinners and neighbors. The only difference is that we have surrendered to the grace of God. I'm suggesting not that we should ignore the reality of their sinfulness, but rather that we prioritize love, kindness, and compassion over condemnation. We should work toward fostering connections that are anchored in authentic love, devoid of pretentious self-righteousness or unhelpful labels.

Ultimately love, not judgment, is the driving force behind true transformation.[18]

Under the Spotlight

In addition to reaching people across the spectrum of religious affiliation, from evangelicals to nones to dones, the church I serve has built relationships with some who do not share the same sexual ethic as we do. This was far easier when our church was smaller and out of the spotlight of public scrutiny.

Once we became affiliated with a well-known global church, the pressure to define our church relative to this one single issue was overwhelming.

Our church may not have been as transparent about our convictions as some other churches were because of our global senior pastor's love for people and his reluctance to see them separated and rejected for their beliefs. We were struggling with how to retain a loving attitude toward people who hold diverse beliefs about sexuality while simultaneously being committed to providing a "welcome home" environment for everyone. We were (and continue to be) convinced that the Holy Spirit convicts us of sin and empowers us to be transformed into the image of Jesus. We were attempting to take a biblical yet humane stance.[19]

For several years, we endeavored to keep this issue out of the pulpit and in the context of personal discipleship conversations where people could hear our truth and our tone in compassionate conversation. We wanted to stay focused on leading people into personal transformation through individual conversations. All the while, the pressure was mounting. Both sides were pushing for us to take a stance. Cancel culture was coming for us from every direction.

During the most intense scrutiny of our global church, and while the issue of same-sex marriage was being hotly debated in Australia, I preached on showing kindness, compassion, and acceptance to the other at our global staff retreat. Although there were more than a thousand staff members in the room, you could have heard a pin drop. It wasn't resistance; it was a sense of everyone listening with an open heart and a desire to get it right. I didn't mention any of the issues surrounding same-gender relationships and marriage, and yet, because of what our church was dealing with at the time, the message was heard through that lens.

A couple of years later, I was in a conversation with our senior pastor, and he referenced that message. He hesitated for a minute, unable to recall the title, before referring to it as "your *gay* message." It was an awkward joke, but I know why he phrased it that way. We didn't know how to discuss the issue of loving the other without it being centered on this *one* defining issue, despite the fact that we live in a world of others—other religions, other races, other philosophies, other issues. When it came to the "same-sex issue," we were caught in the tension of wanting to lead with loving conversations in a religious culture that demands a dogmatic sound bite. It was an unsettling period, and the sense of discomfort over this issue has only intensified in many circles. I don't have a universal solution for every church navigating this conversation other than to suggest that we must find a way to express the virtues of Jesus while representing biblical values.

A steadfast commitment to engage others with kindness and compassion, and to represent their viewpoints honestly and accurately, serves as the foundation for any relationship. An unwillingness to form relationships with people whose beliefs diverge from our own beliefs, or even oppose it, results in a small world and an unproductive life and ministry. This openhearted approach not only expands our understanding of others but also fosters character development within us. We create a fuller, flourishing life and ministry through interacting across ideological divides.

Perhaps the most serious issue we face when it comes to the tension between alternative communities and the church relates to the concern that some people are working to indoctrinate our children. Clearly, there *are* activists who believe biblical values are harmful to children and they feel responsible to deconvert them. There are some people who seek to use our children as pawns to achieve their broader social agendas. In some ways, this is nothing new. I grew up with neighbors who were convinced that I was deprived because my parents didn't smoke, drink, or even own a television, and they made it their business to introduce me to those things. (While those vices are small in comparison to the stakes our children face today, the corollary is valid.) We *should* remain vigilant when it comes to nurturing our children in the ways of the Lord, but without descending into fear and hostility. This moment in the culture is the perfect opportunity to teach our children how to remain strong in the faith and winsome in their witness. We can model for our children what it means to live a life "rooted and grounded in love."[20]

Fear demonizes the other.

Fear paralyzes our love.

Fear magnifies our anxieties and multiplies our anger.

Fear reduces God's saving and sustaining grace to something weak and ineffective.

Fear had no place in the way Jesus interacted with others. He led with love, treating each person as a beloved child of God, lost or found. Perfect love casts out fear with the same force of goodness and grace that he used in expelling demons.

Prejudice always distorts our perception.

If we can't see people through the eyes of love, we will never be able to reach them with the love of God. No one is drawn to God's love by the forces of hate. Shame and condemnation are not effective outreach strategies. That's been proven time and time again. So why do we keep trying them? Why do we keep commending ourselves for our public outrage on the basis of "standing for truth" when God calls us to lay down our lives in love? The way of love is not easy, and I acknowledge that the issues are much more complicated than I can address in a sound bite. Or even in a book. The call to lay down our lives while upholding our truths doesn't allow for us to hide behind sound bites, subtweets, and inhumane conclusions.

The Gospels describe Jesus having dinner with a whole group of different sinners whom their culture would have labeled with scarlet letters. And as unlikely as it may have seemed to the religious leaders, many of them became his followers, because Jesus invested time in building authentic relationships with them.[21]

What moves a person from unlikely to likely?

A few dinners?

A few dinners that lead to deeper conversations?

A few dinners each year over the course of decades?

What if it means you showing up at a bar mitzvah? An iftar? A christening? A wedding? I can't answer these questions for you, and neither can you answer them for me, but it leads to an important point. Loving people will lead us into uncomfortable places and spaces.

If we dine with others through a lifetime only to see them surrender to the love of Jesus in the end, is it worth it? I don't think anyone would hesitate to say yes without question. But what if we attend a lifetime of dinner parties and they never receive our gospel? Is it still worth it? I think the same answer applies. Absolutely. Recently, a young lady in our church crawled into a hospital bed with her ninety-year-old grandmother and led her in a prayer of surrender to Jesus in the final moments of her life. This was after her grandmother ridiculed her faith for years. The only thing that made that possible was her willingness to keep showing up—to stay present and engaged. You never know what might happen if you are willing to go the distance with someone.

Considering this should make us question whether we have a deep, rich, and abiding faith that is strong enough to endure time, hardship, and even persecution to bear fruit in the lives of those we are called to love.

chapter 7

politics, pandemics, and polarization

embracing the way of the kingdom

"Sir," the woman said, "I can see that you are a prophet."

—John 4:19

A decade ago, I received an invitation to speak at an online conference, sponsored by Leadership Network, called The NINES. The theme was "Culture Crash: When Church and Culture Collide." No one then had any idea how much would come crashing down in the years that followed. The question the conveners were trying to answer was this: How does the church handle the hot-button issues that divide Christians from the communities they are assigned to reach and from each other? And the topics we were assigned to address related to the church's position on homosexuality, inclusivity, same-sex marriage, immigration, and the legalization of marijuana.

I accepted the invitation. Looking back, I can't help but wonder, "What in the world was I thinking when I said yes?"

I'm a fifth-generation pastor, and I'm pretty sure my grandfather would be shocked to hear the topics we are discussing in pastoral ministry today. Yet what they discussed at conferences in his day felt just as provocative to them at the time. And as provocative as the "Culture Crash" topics seem to us, two or three generations from now they will seem as tame as the topics my grandfather discussed seem to me now.

In the decade or so since that online conference, the church and the culture's conversations around social issues have become more and more complex. And they're not going to get any simpler in the coming years. Tomorrow's pastors will face unprecedented ethical dilemmas related to technology, genetic engineering, artificial intelligence, and virtual reality as well as the ongoing challenges of racism, sexism, and classism. One of my esteemed seminary professors consistently challenges his students to anticipate the issues tomorrow's pastors may face, such as weddings between humans and artificial intelligence and the ethics of genetic engineering.

Although the issues our society grapples with change from one generation to the next, our inclination toward division remains constant. There was a time when division wasn't championed as a virtue. That time seems distant now. Society stands deeply divided, and there's an alarming pride associated with this state. Division can arise from almost any distinction among people, be it the dynamics of power, race, sexual orientation, political affiliation, or religious belief. These differences are natural and even expected within a democratic society. Differences of opinion lay the foundation for dialogue, which in turn can foster growth. But when we eschew such dialogue, our differences harden into divisions. These divisions become treacherous when they deepen to such an extent that each side becomes stubbornly rooted and perceives the other as an enemy. The deeper we embed ourselves within the confines of our own stance, the higher the barrier between "us" and "them." Given the right conditions, division breeds polarization.

Polarization arises from various factors, including political institutions, ideological divisions, economic inequalities, racial injustices, online echo chambers, and even shifting demographics. In a polarized society, individuals tend to entrench themselves in their views and resist considering alternative perspectives. Hostility between groups increases, and a willingness to compromise for the common good diminishes.

Research on political polarization reveals that exposure to conflicting information can reinforce entrenched views. This is known as the backfire effect. People often seek out information that confirms their beliefs while avoiding contradicting perspectives, further deepening their entrenchment. The way information is shared and consumed, particularly through social media, allows people to surround themselves with like-minded people and ignore diverse opinions.

As groups become more entrenched in their ideologies, they distance themselves from opposing sides, straining societal cohesion. Polarizing rhetoric demonizes and condemns the other group, making attempts to reach out seem like betrayals. The increasing polarization leads to harsh judgments, stereotypes, and demonization between political parties. A 2016 Pew poll found that 47 percent of Republicans thought Democrats were more immoral than non-Democrats, and 35 percent of Democrats felt that way about Republicans. In 2022 those numbers rose to 72 percent and 63 percent, respectively.[1] We are as entrenched as we have ever been in our ideological silos.

Unfortunately, polarization has infiltrated religious institutions as well; everything, including church, is interpreted through the lens of Left and Right. Churches face departures from people who perceive them as either too liberal or too conservative. But the church's responsibility is to preach the gospel of the kingdom and its corresponding values without aligning itself with either end of the political spectrum.

The faith community should value diversity of thought and encourage respectful dialogue and collaboration between conservatives and progressives for the greater good. This fosters a deeper understanding of the gospel and its implications while considering different perspectives and experiences within the community.

Regrettably, fewer people seem willing to put the ideals of unity and love into practice, as is evident in the reluctance to sit next to someone with a different political ideology in church. This division contradicts our faith's core principles, which emphasize that we are one in Christ despite our political views. The emphasis on political beliefs over unity and love highlights a loss of sight within our faith community.

The growing entrenchment is fueled by the idolization

of identity, which prioritizes individualism over collective humanity. This excessive focus on individual identity hampers the well-being of oneself and others and minimizes the importance of our shared humanity. Individualism, while promoting personal growth and innovation, also perpetuates social isolation, selfishness, and a disregard for the well-being of others.

This individualistic mindset fosters a culture of consumerism and materialism, urging people to prioritize personal desires above others' needs. It diminishes empathy and concern for social issues such as poverty, inequality, discrimination, and prejudice. As a result, social cohesion and community suffer.

A healthy balance between individualism and collectivism is crucial for a flourishing community. Recognizing the interdependence of people and understanding that individual and collective interests can coexist is vital. By shifting our focus from individual identities to our shared identity as the *imago Dei*, we find common ground for relational connections and engage in civil, kind, and respectful conversations. It requires relinquishing the idol of individual identities and embracing our shared humanity.

Extremes and Alternatives

Jesus and the Samaritan woman also lived in a highly polarized society. The Jews and Samaritans were profoundly divided, and each was entrenched in their opposition toward the other. During Jesus' day, most Jews went to great lengths to avoid Samaritans, even if it meant going long distances. But Jesus chose a different path, straight through the heart of Samaria. Most Jews wouldn't even acknowledge Samaritans, yet Jesus sought out the Samaritan woman. Most Jews would mock the Samaritans' religion; Jesus, on the other hand, engaged in a meaningful conversation about religious differences.

As the world thinks in *extremes*, the people of God have to think in *alternatives*. The third way exists not in the middle of the extremes but above them. We are called to live not at the center of a Left-Right political world but rather in accordance with the values of God's kingdom. We are ambassadors of a heavenly realm and are called to represent the life of that realm amid the kingdoms of this world.

Though I have spent four decades studying the kingdom of God as the alternative way and my theology has grown and matured over time, I was first introduced to the concept of the "third way" through the writings and lectures of Timothy Keller. In his classic work *Center Church: Doing Balanced, Gospel-Centered Ministry in Your City*, Keller presented his philosophy of the third way and applied it to ecclesiology. He contended that the church should be the center of society, not a fringe institution, and that Christians should engage and understand culture while addressing community issues in accordance with the gospel. He emphasized that the gospel should be central to all the church does, having an impact on both personal salvation and societal transformation.

According to Keller, the third way calls for a fusion of truth and love. He believed the church must be able to articulate the truth in love, cultivating a nuanced approach that does not diminish one for the sake of the other. This involves a courageous willingness to confront sin and error, paired with a profound commitment to extend compassion and grace to those in need, fostering a holistic ministry that resonates with the essence of Christ's teachings. I've served in ministry long enough to watch the tail wag the dog more often than not when it comes to how to do ministry. There's a reason the writers of the New Testament were largely silent on ministry praxis, choosing to remain focused on the higher ideals. I know some may argue that the praxis was already defined since Christianity was born in the seedbed of Judaism and many of the methodologies and practices continued into the first-century church. Despite that, as the church expanded throughout the nations, it encountered new challenges and opportunities, but the higher ideals remained; the Sermon on the Mount was the way Jesus modeled for them.

The philosophical Twitter (now called X) debates surrounding "third wayism" have exploded during the past few years, and though I respect everyone's right to a viewpoint, it hasn't changed my commitment to engage my community with a winsome, missional, gospel-centered approach. I'll let my fruit continue to bear witness to the fact that the people I encounter daily are starved for kindness and compassion.

In a *New York Times* interview regarding his book *Losing Our Religion: An Altar Call for Evangelical America*, Russell Moore observes a shift in why people are losing faith or leaving the church.[2] He notes that previously, individuals often cited disbelief in the supernatural or objections to the church's strict morality, particularly regarding sexual ethics. Now Moore encounters a sense that people view the gospel as a means to an end, such as political or cultural influence, rather than an end in itself. There's growing doubt not about the church being too strict but about whether it adheres to morality at all. Alarmingly, those expressing despair include individuals who were once deeply committed to Christian teachings.

Addressing the crisis within the church, Moore offers a solution I resonate with. He believes the path forward requires a "reordering of priorities," where "ultimate things" are seen as ultimate, and other concerns follow behind. Moore emphasizes the importance of aligning our priorities and loves with the true understanding of what it means to follow Christ. Contrary to a "frantic, angry culture warrior," Moore portrays the figure of Jesus in the New Testament gospels as "remarkably tranquil about the situation around him." He advocates for more of this peacefulness, suggesting that if neighbors saw Christians loving and forgiving one another, regardless of how they viewed theological beliefs, "that would be a good start."

My closest neighbors in the high-rise are not culture warriors seeking to redefine America. They don't despise Christianity, they are perplexed by it. This confusion stems primarily from witnessing distorted expressions of Christianity characterized by clenched teeth, bulging veins, and raised fists from individuals who claim to represent the faith. They were horrified to see "Jesus placards" raised in protest during the January 6 insurrection and the blasphemous prayers made on the US Senate chamber floor by those who advocated for violence and the hanging of the vice president. They also witnessed firsthand in Arizona the intolerance exhibited by those who have conflated Christianity with civil religion.

One might argue in response to the previous sentence that it is those at the other end of the political spectrum who express intolerance toward many values connected to our

Judeo-Christian heritage. I do not dispute this. Both sides exhibit intolerance and contribute to the polarization we see. My intention is merely to propose that the responsibility to exemplify the virtues of Jesus lies with the people of God; we shouldn't expect an unbelieving world to do so. While engaging in debates and disagreements, lobbying, and voting to shape the community we desire for our children, let us do so with a gentle, peaceful, and receptive spirit as our foundation.[3]

The Third Way

Instead of allowing ourselves to be forced into factions, Christians need to forge our own path through the complex issues of our day—following the way of Jesus. The kingdom alternative exists as a higher ideal, a more virtuous and noble path, than the ways of tribalism and its corresponding fruit of division and destruction.

Gerald Sittser has written extensively about how the early Christians didn't conform to either of the two opposing sides of their culture—the way of Rome or the way of Judaism. In his book *Resilient Faith: How the Early Christian "Third Way" Changed the World*, he describes their approach as an alternative to the middle ground. Long before Timothy Keller popularized the idea of the third way, the alternative way of Jesus was embedded in the church and described as early as the second century.[4]

The third way means seeking the kingdom alternative for the sake of the common good of humanity. Instead of fighting culture wars against either side, early Christians spent their time creating a countercultural community, serving the marginalized, and sharing the news of Jesus' resurrection. Today, however, instead of loving and serving the communities in which they are situated, many Christians have undermined the credibility of the gospel by cuddling the king in an attempt to curry his favor. Their naked ambition for social capital and political power position them more effectively as culture warriors rather than ambassadors of the kingdom of God. Culture warriors rarely make for kingdom ambassadors, since ambassadors are by definition those sent on a mission with a message of peace.

There is a marked difference between the posture of a culture warrior, who is generally focused on conquering, versus that of an ambassador, who is dedicated to representing and persuading. Warriors deepen divisions while ambassadors cross borders. Warriors seek the hard power of strength and control, while ambassadors use the soft power of kindness, connection, and friendship. Warriors bring war, but ambassadors bring an offer of peace and harmony.

The early Christians were less about transforming Rome and more about serving as ambassadors of Jesus' kingdom. Their commitment to this third way was starkly demonstrated during a devastating plague that wiped out a fifth of the Roman Empire's population. Death was everywhere, with bodies piled up in the streets of major cities like Rome. This catastrophe didn't just affect the populace's health, it wreaked havoc on the economy and societal structures: cities were reduced to ruins, starvation became rampant, commerce halted, and even military forces found themselves immobilized.

In the midst of this devastating pandemic, the church embodied the grace of Jesus. Many Christian leaders of the era penned poignant letters describing the church's stance during this crisis, their words now ranking among the most inspiring accounts ever written. Sittser's reflections shed light on the scenario: "The Christian faith made a practical difference in the lives of the people, offering hope in the face of acute suffering and calling people to serve the afflicted. In general, Christians faced the plagues with courage, nursed the sick, and buried the dead. They believed that because God loved them, as undeserving as they were, they were duty-bound to love others."[5]

The disparity between this response and the reactions of many evangelicals during the COVID-19 pandemic is striking. While it's critical to avoid overgeneralization, because not everyone responded identically, it was observed that a significant number of people reacted similarly, hinting at what historical records might depict in the future.

They panicked when the virus appeared.
They divided from one another and the communities
    they once professed love for.
They prioritized their "rights" over caring for others.
They politicized a global health crisis.
They spread disinformation about the origin of the virus
    and the potential treatment.
They doubled down on their deeply entrenched
    ideological positions.
They still sang their songs to Jesus as if nothing had
    changed.

Instead of responding with practical help and care for the vulnerable the way the early church did, too many Christians on both ends of the political spectrum dug down even deeper into their trenches. The pandemic polarized our world even further, and the church was no exception. When my church moved to online worship, one side accused us of being compromisers who had stepped on the slippery slope toward the eradication of our faith. Then when we gathered back in person with health guidelines in place, the other side accused us of putting peoples' health at risk. We were in a no-win situation, pulled by polarizing forces on both sides of every issue. And so was every other church in the world.

It would be tempting for the church to look at these two extremes in our polarized culture and desire to find a middle ground. The moderate middle may seem like it's the solution for a church trying to unify people and keep the peace, but the middle is where you get crucified for not taking a stand. The third way, the kingdom alternative, is not about embracing centrism. It is not about finding the "golden mean," as Aristotle described it; it's about a radically different way of living based on the teachings of Jesus.

No one who has ever read the Gospels would describe Jesus as the moderate middle. Not the Jesus who turned over tables, tore down dividing walls, challenged the status quo, and crossed dividing lines like a "scab" in the middle of a strike. He was anything but a centrist. He didn't sit in the middle of two extremes in an effort to avoid controversy. He didn't condescend to Right-Left dichotomies; instead, he was committed to righteousness and justice, regardless of which group happened to also be aligned with those values in any moment. Ultimately, he offended everyone equally in his mission to proclaim and embody the coming of God's new kingdom.

Jesus was a countercultural revolutionary who challenged the systems of his day, and we, too, as his ambassadors, should strive to do the same in the spirit of his teachings.

My Story

I can't share about the perils of politics, pandemics, and polarization without telling you about how these themes have shaped the past three years of my life. Since nothing is wasted in God's plan, I know that the hard lessons of these years are meant to be shared.

In 2019, our church was bursting at the seams. It was an outstanding year for us. From our humble beginnings in a community center two decades earlier, we had grown to encompass seven locations and an active congregation of 8,500 people. Special events swelled us to more than 10,000, and our weekly Sunday-night service was the picture of the revival-like atmosphere I had always dreamed of being a part of. Every Sunday night more than a thousand young adults gathered to worship, with many crowding the altars, creating a mosh pit of joyful exuberant worship.

Then we established our global church's only extension Leadership College outside Australia and immediately had two hundred students enrolled in daily classes, serving the church's mission in the evenings and on the weekends. Our church was enjoying our best days completely oblivious to the storm that was brewing.

That's not to say we were without challenges. The 2016 election season had exposed some underlying tensions within our local community and our global church. As disconcerting as they were, I'd hoped that time, faithfulness to the gospel, and the fruitfulness of a growing church would heal those fissures. Little did I realize that the fissures were going to crack wide open, like the earth during the shifting of tectonic plates, and that we were going to be facing chasms within our congregation.

The first real sign of the impending conflict was in late fall 2019 when I received a surprise call from our global senior pastor inviting me to join him in a visit to the White House to meet with President Trump. This wasn't unfamiliar territory; I'd attended the National Prayer Breakfast a couple of times and was even recognized for my leadership of Arizona 1.27, our statewide foster care ministry.

Interestingly, this was my second White House invitation. The first was in 2014, to meet President Obama. An unexpected international crisis led to a last-minute cancellation, but the news of my intent to meet him still evoked criticism by those in our church who were opposed to his policies.

The invitation to meet President Trump elicited opposition, including from within my own family. Concerns were raised that this meeting might be perceived as an endorsement of the president's divisive views on women, minorities, and immigrants—views that starkly contrast with our own. However, I hoped to engage with the president without endorsing his politics, much like I engage with individuals from diverse backgrounds without condoning their actions. Rooted in the belief that God calls us to be gracious to everyone, irrespective of their political or lifestyle choices, I accepted the invitation. I saw it as an opportunity to be a light in the darkness, akin to figures like Joseph in Egypt, Daniel in Babylon, or Paul engaging with Roman power. Except, of course, my attendance was voluntary.

Years of service on Arizona governor's councils and as the chair of a statewide task force have taught me the value of bipartisanship for the greater good of our communities. Having served four Arizona governors—two Republicans and two Democrats—I believe that avoiding people with differing political ideologies narrows our world and limits opportunities to best serve the community.

The White House event was eye opening in many ways.

Upon arrival, we convened in the Eisenhower Building for an hour of prayer and worship. Despite my reservations about the administration, I was profoundly moved by a genuine and palpable sense of God's presence during our devotional time. Following another hour of remarks from the vice president, the secretary of state, and other cabinet members, we were escorted to the Cabinet Room just off the Rose Garden. Once there, the atmosphere shifted abruptly; many who had seemed enraptured by God's presence moments earlier began aggressively jockeying for a prominent position next to the president.

The next half hour was a blur as the president commented on the economy, his view of the erosion of religious liberties, and his appreciation for the support of the evangelical community. At the conclusion of his remarks, as if on a whim, he looked around the room and asked, "Would you like to see my office?" The murmur of affirmation around the table made it clear: we all wanted to see the Oval Office.

Entering the Oval Office from the Cabinet Room was a surreal experience, one I will never forget. Despite disagreeing with the president's rhetoric and personal conduct, I felt an unexpected surge of raw ambition. To my surprise, in that moment, I *wanted* to be in that room, surrounded by the trappings of power, standing next to the most powerful politician on the planet. Though it's a story for another time, let me be clear about one thing: the allure of power targets any vulnerabilities within our souls. If we don't consistently embody the cruciform life, shaped by the self-sacrificing love and humility of Jesus, our unguarded moments can easily be overtaken by unchecked ambition, replacing Christ's nature with our self-interest.

As quickly as ambition rose within me, it was met with a sense of conviction about my hypocrisy.

As we crowded around the Resolute desk jostling for position to be next to be photographed with President Trump, I suddenly heard the whisper of the Holy Spirit penetrating my struggle and the surrounding chatter, echoing the words of the twenty-third Psalm."The LORD is my shepherd; I shall not want."[6]

Those nine words soothed my heightened state like drops of cool water. I clung to that line like a drowning man clinging to a life preserver, repeating it over and over in my thoughts as a form of defiance against the principalities and powers trying to drown me. That passage kept me from being swept away by the moment and anchored me in the source of God's provision and power. *I don't need worldly power because my heavenly Shepherd has provided what I need.*

Later that day, following our visit to the Oval Office, we were each emailed an official photograph of our meeting with the president along with guidelines on appropriate uses.

Within moments, all of those restrictions were disregarded as several of the other people in attendance posted the photo on their social-media pages, church websites, and, in one case, their own political campaign press release.

Many people saw the photograph and assumed the intentions of each person pictured there. In the eyes of the public, my physical presence equated to a political endorsement. Where one side would judge and vilify me for expressing pastoral care toward people whose lifestyles they disagreed with, the other side would come down equally as harshly against my visit to the White House. Yet in both circumstances I was simply trying to bear witness to something greater than our distinctions and divisions—the grace of a loving God.

How often do we judge others based on a single moment, a snapshot, without considering the full context or the person's intentions? What does that say about our willingness to understand and empathize?

The photograph captured in December 2019 marked the beginning of a series of crises for our church. The first crisis emerged as a result of a cancel culture that presumed guilt without considering the possibility of innocence. Shortly thereafter, the COVID-19 pandemic struck, introducing the second crisis. In the summer of 2020, the unfinished work of the civil rights movement converged with calls for justice from people of color, giving rise to the third crisis. As if that weren't enough, later in 2020 a fourth crisis threatened to overwhelm our church when one of the other lead pastors was exposed for infidelity. These successive waves of pandemics left us breathless as we struggled to comprehend the rapid and profound changes that had taken place in our world.

Most of all, I was stunned at just how quickly those four crises led to polarization within our church. It happened in the blink of an eye. Of course, we now know there were a thousand fissures in the groundwork of our communities and the polarization was not created overnight. These conflicts simply revealed the issues that were just beneath the surface.

The third crisis presented another photo-induced controversy that reverberated throughout my life and ministry. As you will recall, civil protests swept across the nation following the murder of George Floyd. Despite building our church for two decades on the biblical principles of racial reconciliation, we were caught in the crossfire. On the one hand, frustration boiled over among those who were weary of witnessing the repeated and brutal victimization of young Black men. Conversely, another faction denied systemic racism, maintaining that the civil rights movement had ended and that law enforcement remained beyond reproach. Like most other churches, we found ourselves enveloped in the conflict.

Early in the summer protests, I was informed of a massive crowd spontaneously gathering in the street between our downtown cathedral and parking lot. Concerned for their safety and that of our campus security, and mindful of our proximity to police headquarters and the potential for violence, I raced to the scene. On arrival, I invited the protest organizers into our parking lot. Before long, hundreds swelled into thousands as the call for justice rang out louder and louder, echoing off the high-rise buildings and down the corridor of our streets.

The protest organizers, struggling to be seen and heard above the clamor, asked for permission to climb onto a towering piece of heavy construction machinery. Perched high above the crowd, they poured out their pain through a megaphone using passionate and combative language. For more than an hour, they rallied the crowd with chants calling for reform.

Standing there in that surreal moment, looking at the sea of humanity against the background of the cathedral, which has stood as a landmark for a century, I heard someone calling for me over the megaphone.

"Would the pastor come up here and pray for us?"

Swallowing hard, I climbed onto the vehicle, took the megaphone, and found myself repenting for our national sins, an act as unexpected as it was unplanned.

"God forgive us for the way we have sinned against you and each other."

For a moment, the crowd went silent.

Heads were bowed.

Protest signs were lowered.

And the grace of God flooded the street.

Public repentance is the first step to social redemption.

As society becomes increasingly characterized by anger, outrage, and hostility, the people of God should stand out as the alternative. One moment of humility opened a door into a community I never could have entered on any other basis. This reflects the power and reach of empathy, demonstrating how a single act can bridge seemingly insurmountable divides.

When we bridge divides, we strengthen communities.

As I prayed over the crowd, megaphone in hand, a photojournalist captured the moment. The aftermath was another wave of knee-jerk judgment. Within weeks, hundreds of members left our church; only a handful cared to question my involvement. Many, whom I had led to Jesus and ministered to for years, let their political agendas overshadow my pastoral presence. Their allegiance to conservative politics appeared stronger than their commitment to their church community. These were people who worshiped alongside our members of color, affirmed my teaching on racial reconciliation, and even celebrated our national holidays affirming minorities. None of that mattered as the surge of polarization pushed them to the margins.

The image with President Trump sparked progressive outrage.

The photo at the Black Lives Matter rally triggered conservative backlash.

Witnessing the departure of beloved church members was agonizing, yet I remain unable to conceive an alternative. Following Jesus means living a life of sacrifice, bearing the cross, and bracing for rejection. I live and lead conscious that one day I'll answer to Jesus for my decisions. And so will you.[7]

Living according to the values and practices of God's kingdom isn't easy to do. And that's a gross understatement. The kingdom way is difficult and costly. It demands a courage that doesn't come easily. It exacts a heavy price as all sides demand conformity to their will and way. Embracing the third way isn't about sidestepping controversy; it's a conscious choice to do hard things motivated by the firm conviction that the kingdom way is the only way that matters in the end.

When examining the adherence of early Christians to the third way, it becomes evident that their focus extended beyond mere lifestyle or discipleship formation. Instead, it centered on a profound understanding of the very fabric of reality and the central figure within it—Jesus Christ. The third way emerged as a natural consequence of their unwavering belief in him as the core of their existence.

Seeing how Jesus lived and died should frame the nature of our engagement with the world.

He taught us to love our enemies, pray for those who persecute us, and forgive those who wrong us.[8] In this way, his example teaches us that our engagement with the world should be rooted in love, kindness, compassion, and forgiveness, rather than anger, judgment, or condemnation.

As followers of Jesus, it falls upon us to present an alternative paradigm of engagement, particularly on contentious social issues, regardless of our deep-seated convictions. By focusing on shared values, engaging in respectful discourse, and working collaboratively, we can coexist peacefully. Listening to diverse perspectives, engaging the community, and upholding a clear understanding of the gospel can help us navigate divisive issues with grace and respect.

How have you reacted when faced with unjust criticism or misinterpretation of your actions? What did these experiences teach you about the importance of context, communication, and courage?

chapter 8

a tale of two mountains

divided by race, united in love

"Our ancestors worshiped on this mountain, but you Jews claim that the place where we must worship is in Jerusalem." "Woman," Jesus replied, "believe me, a time is coming when you will worship the Father neither on this mountain nor in Jerusalem."
—John 4:20–21

Standing at the base of the mountain, I gazed up in awe. At six years old, I was used to being small, but nothing could have prepared me for how it would feel to look at the massive sculpture of Presidents Washington, Jefferson, Roosevelt, and Lincoln looming large in front of me. This was my first visit to Mount Rushmore. It was breathtaking.

My dad had recently graduated from Bible college and moved our family to the Black Hills of South Dakota to plant a church. The Black Hills are best known for Mount Rushmore, where the heads of the presidents stand sixty feet tall, carved into the granite mountain. It took fourteen years for Gutzon Borglum to skillfully blast them into existence. And more than three million tourists visit the site each year.

The property that Mount Rushmore occupies was originally owned by the Lakota tribe of the Great Sioux Nation. The Treaty of Fort Laramie (1868) granted the Black Hills to the Lakota in perpetuity, but the US seized the area from them after the Great Sioux War of 1876.

It was never given back.

My family had arrived in South Dakota in 1971, just after the American Indian Movement occupied Mount Rushmore to protest the injustice of losing their lands. John Fire Lame Deer, a Native American "holy man, led young activists, grandparents, and children to the top of the mountain, where he planted a Lakota prayer staff. He said that the presidents' faces would 'remain dirty until the treaties concerning the Black Hills are fulfilled.'"[1]

On that first visit to Mount Rushmore, I heard the story of the activists who were removed a few months earlier. Even though I was only six, I felt really strange about it. I was sad. I wondered why the "Indians" couldn't have their land. I wondered why we couldn't find a way to share it. I wondered why we had taken it from them in the first place.

What added to the conflict in my soul was the fact that just seventeen miles away there was another granite mountain being sculpted. It was of a Lakota riding on a horse. His name was Crazy Horse. His sculpture was taking forever to complete. In fact, it took just fourteen years to sculpt four presidents onto Mount Rushmore, but it has taken more than seventy years to sculpt just the face of Crazy Horse—with no end to the project in sight.

The contrast between those two mountains set the context in my young soul for the disparities and divisions I would see in my childhood in South Dakota between the Sioux Nation and the white community—and later in the Deep South between the Black and white communities.

From my earliest memories, I've held a deep-seated passion for racial reconciliation—for opportunity and equality and equity extended to those who are disadvantaged.

I am still a learner in this conversation.

We all are, regardless of our color.

Recent years have proven that we all have a long way to go when it comes to healing the racial wounds of the past four hundred years. The summer of 2020 was a grim reminder of our painful past and our unresolved present. Following the public murders of Ahmaud Arbery and George Floyd in the spring of that year, the nation erupted in sorrow, confusion, outrage, and despair that summer. It was a brutal reminder of how much work lies ahead of us to build a fair and just society.

The immediate aftermath of Floyd's murder included widespread protests in cities across the country. These protests, which were primarily led by Black activists and allies, called for an end to police violence and systemic racism. The protests were sparked by the graphic video of Floyd's death, which showed Officer Chauvin, who is white, kneeling on Floyd's neck for nearly nine minutes, despite Floyd's pleas that he couldn't breathe. The video, which was widely shared on social media, served as a powerful catalyst for the protests, which spread quickly from Minneapolis to other cities across the United States and around the world.

Whether you believe the blame is to be laid at the feet of politics, police, or protesters, I think most of us—Black, white, Asian, Hispanic, and Indigenous—would agree that we aren't as far along as we had hoped as it relates to equality and opportunity for all people.

And if things are bad in the nation, they are not much better in the church. Yes, there are Christians faithfully laboring behind the scenes to love their neighbors and connect with people of different ethnicities, but overall the way we have approached this issue leaves a lot to be desired. Even worse, we seem to be moving away from each other in increasing ways. At the moment I am writing this paragraph, 86 percent of all churches in America show no significant racial diversity.

The message that we convey to the world does not express kindness, compassion, and generosity.

When it comes to the deep-seated racial divisions in our nation, we often get Charles Spurgeon's dictum backward: we are making soft arguments using hard words.

There are two extremes to this conversation taking place at this moment in our world. On one side, there are those who are deeply passionate about fighting the issue of racial injustice. They believe it is systemic and that those who hold power are bent on intentionally perpetuating it. They believe that every white person is guilty of either contributing to white supremacy or benefiting from it.

On the other side, there are those who believe that racial

injustice no longer exists in society. They think the civil rights movement resolved the last vestiges of structural racism; therefore, any experience with racism is unusual, exaggerated, or contrived to benefit individuals who already have equal opportunities.

I think most people who love Jesus, his gospel, and his church—who want to be faithful to the mission to love God and neighbor—are between those two extremes. *Maybe I'm wrong about that, but let me cling to some hope.* Most of us are seeking a better way—the kingdom way—instead of the way proposed by political extremes. We're just trying to figure it out in a way that is charitable, equitable, and, most important, faithful to the Scriptures. The full manifestation of a church that models the beauty and diversity of heaven eludes us, but that doesn't mean we give up on the dream of seeing it realized. The work of reconciliation is never easy; it comes at great cost. As we wrestle with our explicit and implicit biases, we must lean heavily on the hope of sanctification. Whether you stand on one side or another of the political spectrum, or are seeking the third way, each of us must continually make room for the gospel to do a deep work in our hearts.

Worship Wars

One can draw parallels between the historical relationship between Samaritans and Jews and the current state of race relations between Black and white people. And there is some correlation, because both groups have a deep history of pain and layers of animosity that have built up over the centuries. Judgment and hatred and power struggles are common themes in both stories. The difference is that the division between the Samaritans and Jews was primarily rooted in religious differences. It was supported by racial and ethnic distinctions, but religion was at the heart of the conflict. Nonetheless, by overcoming that division with grace and love, Jesus provided us with a road map for navigating differences of any kind.

The Samaritans worshiped on one mountain—Mount Gerizim, right outside Shechem—and the Jews worshiped on another—Mount Zion, in Jerusalem. Remember, the Northern Kingdom of Israel (from which the Samaritans were descended, mixed with gentiles) and the Southern Kingdom of Judah (from which the Jews were descended) were originally one nation—Israel. The one nation of twelve tribes whom God brought out of slavery in Egypt into the promised land.

When Joshua brought that second generation of Israelites into the promised land, he renewed the covenant with God outside Shechem, between two mountains, Mount Gerizim and Mount Ebal. He built an altar on Mount Ebal and offered sacrifices there. Then half the tribes stood on Mount Gerizim to pronounce the blessings of the covenant and the other half stood on Mount Ebal to pronounce the curses of the covenant, just as God had instructed them in the law.[2]

Later, when David became king, he made Jerusalem his capital city and he brought the ark of the covenant there and put it in the tabernacle on the site of Mount Zion.[3] From that point on, Jerusalem and Mount Zion were considered sacred places of worship for Jews. Many of the prophets say that in the eternal kingdom of God all believers from every nation, tribe, and tongue will gather at Mount Zion to worship the

Lord.[4] Including both Judah and Israel, Jews and Samaritans, together.[5]

When the nation split into north and south, Israel and Judah, the Jews continued to worship at Mount Zion, but Jeroboam built two other temples for the Northern Kingdom—one at Dan and one at Bethel. More than 150 years later, when the Assyrians took over the Northern Kingdom and the king of Assyria sent foreign nations to intermarry with the Israelites, a priest was sent to reestablish worship of the Lord at Bethel.[6] Then after almost another 150 years, the Southern Kingdom, Judah, fell to the Babylonians and they were taken into exile for 70 years. When they came back, they rebuilt their temple at Jerusalem. The Samaritans originally offered to help them rebuild it, because they had also been worshiping the Lord. But because they had been worshiping other gods as well, and had intermarried with the gentiles, the leaders of Judah refused their help.[7]

The Samaritans built their own temple on Mount Gerizim, the original site where Joshua had recommitted to the covenant, choosing Mount Gerizim over Mount Ebal because that is the mountain where they pronounced the blessings. About one hundred years before Christ, the Jews destroyed the Samaritan temple at Mount Gerizim, which is considered by scholars to be the final nail in the coffin for the relationship between Jews and Samaritans.[8]

In Jesus' day, the theological controversy continued over the legitimate place to worship: Mount Gerizim or Mount Zion. For the Jews and Samaritans, it was one or the other; their faith didn't allow for a third way. Yet Jesus introduced an alternative, hinting that in the future the location of our worship won't matter because "true worshipers will worship the Father in the Spirit and in truth."[9] He didn't choose one side or the other, and he didn't tell the Samaritan woman that worshipers should meet in the middle, halfway between Mount Gerizim and Mount Zion. He gave her an alternative third way. A whole different way to worship.

In one sentence, Jesus created a path toward healing the division between Jews and Samaritans. He finds a way beyond mountains, through restrictions, and over separations. He points to a future where the people of God reject the sinful practices of previous generations and refuse to let religious, ethnic, or cultural differences separate them.

Jesus' answer must have seemed impossible to the Samaritan woman when she first heard it. Then, a few moments later, she realized that Jesus was the Messiah and accepted him as her Lord and Savior. The gospel broke into her life with a love powerful enough to heal any divide. Suddenly the third way opened in front of her, dissolving long-held resentments and breaking down barriers.

That same life-altering love is available to us today. The gospel provides the hope for racial reconciliation, if we are courageous enough to embrace it.

Diversity and Equity

The racial divide in our nation lingers, and some contend it is as entrenched as it has ever been. Recent events have proven that we are a long way from healing the racial wounds of the past four hundred years. Those championing racial reconciliation are met with resistance and even hostility, often from the most unexpected quarters. Commitment to biblical justice is misconstrued as political correctness or even as aligning with controversial ideologies. Within the conservative Christian community, the alarm over associations with socialism, Marxism, and critical race theory has led to a kind of racial myopia, obstructing our vision and clouding our understanding. Cultural debates and political talking points have diverted attention away from the healing, reconciling love of God. A genuine, unbiased engagement with Scripture, unfettered by cultural influences, should naturally inspire every follower of Christ to strive for a world marked by fairness and equity. Yet we often find ourselves resisting this call or, even worse, ignoring the issue altogether.

My dedication to racial reconciliation runs deep. It is not driven by social theories, a need for cultural approval, or any expression of "wokeism." Instead, it is grounded in the revelation of creation, redemption, new creation, and what it means to truly walk in the way of Jesus. Reconciliation is at the heart of the gospel.

The origin of racial reconciliation is the act of creation itself, where God's vision sculpted a planet imbued with stunning diversity and breathtaking wonder. Rather than crafting a monolithic landscape, God sculpted mountains, valleys, deserts, and rainforests. Instead of a singular form of life, he populated the earth with an astonishing array of nearly nine million species. In creating humanity, God instilled the first humans with the genetic potential for every ethnicity known today, every shade and nuance, every distinct facial feature, and every conceivable form of human beauty. This was God's grand design, a masterpiece reflecting the infinite facets of his divine nature, and it was and remains wondrous in his eyes.

God then instructed humankind to multiply and populate the earth. As people spread and settled in various regions, they adapted to their environments. In colder climates, there was less sun exposure, while warmer conditions fostered the development of melanin, leading to a gradual change in skin tones. This expansion across the globe gave rise to an enriching diversity. Languages evolved, each carrying its own stories and songs, and distinct cultures flourished, each reflecting a facet of human experience and creativity. None of this caught God by surprise.

Diversity was part of his plan from the beginning.

God's delight in diversity is matched only by his anguish over division and injustice. Just as earthly parents revel in the joy of seeing their children get along, so too does our heavenly Father. He yearns for his children to live in unity and grieves when sin drives a wedge between us. Imagine the sorrow he must feel when the diversity he designed for his pleasure and purpose—a clear symbol of his creativity, embedded in our DNA—becomes a source of our division. Racism is a rejection of the inherent beauty in human diversity, leading to division and sinful acts of injustice. Though this sin may begin as a personal bias, it has historically evolved into a structural and institutional issue in many societies, including our own. The seeds of racism, planted in individual hearts, grow to affect entire communities, poisoning minds and relationships along the way. When we neglect to confront this sin at a personal level, it becomes embedded in the fabric of society. This isn't a mere product of modern social theories, it's a manifestation of original sin, with deep roots in the human condition.Sin *is* personal, but it can also be national, systemic, and structural. Fallen people organize societies and perpetuate cycles and systems of brokenness. Throughout the Old Testament, God used the prophets to call the Israelites to corporate repentance for sins like injustice, oppression, usury, and neglect of the poor. We see examples of cities and nations called upon to humble themselves in sackcloth and ashes. No one got a free pass. Everyone had benefited from, contributed to, or perpetuated the communal injustice, so they all had to repent together.

What if ancient Israel had reacted to the prophets' calls for repentance from national sin with the dismissive attitudes we witness today? Imagine if, instead of heeding the warnings of the prophets, they had formed an alliance with devout Jews and neighboring pagan nations to silence both the cries of the suffering and God's mandate to attend to their needs. What if they had ignored the plight of the poor, the oppressed, and the immigrants simply because it contradicted prevailing political sentiment? The Bible we have been entrusted with would likely tell a profoundly different story.[10]

When the ancient Israelites confronted and repented for their national sins, they opened the door for hope and healing. Our response to the recognition of national sin should echo this act of humility and repentance. The process requires not only acknowledgment and sorrow but also a decisive turn away from sin and committed efforts to mend the fractures it has caused. We cannot retreat from this sacred responsibility. Through the cross, we were reconciled to God, and now, we are commissioned to be ambassadors of reconciliation in the world. This ministry extends beyond merely bridging the gap between individuals and God; it encompasses a comprehensive restoration—connecting people to God, healing relationships with self and others, and restoring all of creation to its intended harmony. As followers of Jesus, we are called to be an expression of God's heavenly kingdom here on earth, embodying reconciliation, equality, unity, and promoting human flourishing in every way.

Heartbeat Monitor

Martin Luther King Jr., paraphrasing the words of Theodore Parker, a Harvard theologian, Universalist pastor, and abolitionist, popularized the notion that "the arc of the moral universe is long, but it bends toward justice."[11] Change takes a long time, but it does happen. I'll leave it to others to debate whether that arc bends through the incremental changes of a critical mass or is more forcefully bent by reformers intent on social change, but one thing is clear to me: we will not change what we do not acknowledge.

I have often pondered whether the moral progress of society behaves like a heartbeat monitor—characterized by sudden spikes and drops, with long stretches of inactivity in between. The conversation around racial injustices in society tends to be reactive. While communities of color are constantly affected by systemic racism, white communities tend to ignore the issue until a major injustice brings it to the fore. When we finally acknowledge the problem, there is a brief period of heightened awareness and energy directed toward fighting for justice—a spike. We hold on to hope that this time change will be lasting, but soon enough, attention shifts and the line drops back down. The issue that once seemed so pressing is now ignored once again, until the next injustice jolts us back into awareness.

In recent years, the frequency of these reactive responses has intensified, as the general public has been exposed to the footage of the deaths of people of color. It has become increasingly difficult for white communities to ignore the reality of racism when it is displayed in such graphic detail. Each time we rush in to help, however, our efforts are often met with disappointment.

The moral progress of society can be sustained across generations when followers of Jesus come together to work for biblical justice.

The work of justice is not without opposition, and, in this case, those who oppose it are deeply entrenched among us. Even more, we have been discipled in their thinking. You don't have to look far before you encounter the flawed and harmful ways the church has tried to address racism. The most egregiously sinful response has been outright denial, but promoting color blindness as a virtue runs a close second.

When we talk about race, some people idealistically wonder, "Shouldn't we all just be color-blind? Since everyone is made in the image of God, and since we are all equal in God's eyes, is it even helpful to acknowledge our racial and ethnic distinctions?"

I felt the same way for many years. In my attempt to show love and value and respect for other people, I thought the best thing I could do was to overlook their ethnic distinctions. As much as I thought I was helping, unfortunately I wasn't. I was minimizing the beauty and the uniqueness of those with whom I was attempting to stand as an ally and dismissing the struggles my friends of color deal with every day.

While the idea of being color-blind may seem logical in theory, when you stop to think about it, there are a couple of fundamental problems with seeing color blindness as a helpful practice.

Being color-blind is not what God intended. The concept is not found anywhere in the Bible. In fact, we find the exact opposite. God loves ethnic diversity, and he includes ethnic distinctions as a reminder of his original intent and design. If God wanted to, he could have made us all one color. But he didn't. He is the architect of diversity, and he delights in it. God is glorified through the diverse tapestry of nations, tribes, and tongues. Therefore, color blindness is like telling God, "We are uncomfortable with the way you designed things and we refuse to acknowledge it."

Besides dishonoring God's creativity, color blindness is also dehumanizing. Being color-blind is often used to whitewash (pun intended) the atrocities of the past and ignore the inequalities of the present. Closing our eyes to color results in closing our eyes to the injustice that exists in our world.

As Christians, we are called to go into the world with eyes wide open, to see injustice, so we can proclaim liberty to the captive. Being blind to differences means being blind to the painful realities that some people experience. Denying differences won't make injustice go away, but it will desensitize us to the lived realities of the many people who are discriminated against because of the color of their skin.

Rather than striving for color blindness, it is more

constructive to say, "I see your color, and I recognize the unique challenges you face because of it, challenges I will never personally face. I understand that your color might mean you have to constantly prove yourself in ways I don't. I see the pressure on you to be twice as good to get half the respect. I know that you have to warn your sons about how to behave when they are pulled over by the police. I acknowledge the many hurdles you face daily, simply because of your color, that I will never encounter in my own experience."

It's a statement of privilege even to say, "Why can't we all just be color-blind?"

Refusing to pursue color blindness as an ideal not only glorifies God's design for diversity, but it also honors the struggles, pains, and injustices of our brothers and sisters of color.

Let Love Lead

Regardless of how much we try to do the hard work to understand one another, it's still hard to talk about race across color lines. We are all approaching this from a place of discomfort. Many white people feel guilty over our national atrocities and powerless to change the past and remedy the present. We don't engage because we lack the tools to navigate the conversation. And many people of color have learned what happens when they raise the issue—the blowback is intense.

Conversations create bridges or barricades; what we build depends on the orientation of our heart.

Our only hope to move the conversation forward is to let love lead. The same kind of audacious love that Jesus demonstrated to the Samaritans, the Romans, the Canaanites, all the enemies of the Jews, and every person he encountered, irrespective of their racial or ethnic identities, is what we need to heal the racial divide in our nation.

Love may seem like an easy virtue to rally around since it's the obvious antidote to the vitriol of racism. Yet choosing the way of love is not easy. Even those of us committed to racial reconciliation can struggle to lead with love. When we discuss hot-button issues like racism, our emotions get engaged and our defenses get rattled, and what we excuse as righteous indignation rushes to the surface. Love and loathing rage within us, and, sometimes, loathing wins. In our anger, we spit out harsh words and harbor judgmental thoughts as sharing the love of Christ becomes less important than making our point heard. Or, at least, that's what I have experienced in my efforts to compel people to see a better way.

Several years ago when we were in the planning stage for the launch of our college in Phoenix, I spent an afternoon hosting two of our international faculty members. At one point in the conversation, I raised the issue of promoting equity within the student body by offering scholarships to minorities and identifying and hiring people of color for our faculty. I was unprepared for their curious response. "Slavery was four hundred years ago, the civil rights movement was a century ago, why can't 'these people' just get over it?" Realizing that I was facing a major cultural barrier, I took a deep breath, swallowed my frustration, hit the lock button on the car, and said, "We're going to sit in this car in the middle of the Arizona summer until we have this conversation." For the following hour, in a scorching car where the air conditioner couldn't keep pace with the heat, I shared my perspective on why calling people of color "these people" was wildly inappropriate and how the legacy of racial injustice is nowhere close to being resolved. I've since discovered this question to be far more common than I realized at the time.

Later, as I reflected back on the conversation, I realized that it was easier for me to extend grace to minorities than to those in the majority culture. Understanding that, I have to consistently remind myself that even decent people have been indoctrinated in indecent ways. We are all disciples of the time, place, and context of our personal formation until we see the way of Jesus and become discipled by the message of the kingdom. I have my own blind spots, spiritually unformed areas, and constant need for grace.

When participating in discussions about race, it's important to be prepared for discomfort. We should approach these conversations with humility and a willingness to listen and learn. Instead of ignoring the experiences of those who have faced, and continue to face, discrimination, we should listen to and understand their experiences. This requires an openness to learning and the willingness to say "Teach me."

It is crucial for the majority culture to listen to and acknowledge the experiences of minorities with regards to bias, prejudice, discrimination, and racism, even if it makes us uncomfortable. Listening to the stories of people of color within our communities can be overwhelming and may cause some to avoid the conversation or seek quick solutions to complex historical issues, neither of which is helpful.

The disciples were clearly uncomfortable with Jesus talking to the woman at the well, but he didn't seem moved by their discomfort. He naturally reached across the dividing lines of race, gender, and status to show kindness and compassion. He embraced the messy and uncomfortable to connect with people and meet them where they were.

Navigating the landscape of racial reconciliation is challenging, and I have personally made many mistakes along the way. In my attempts to connect with people of other races and ethnicities, I have said some insensitive things, such as asking Jewish friends how they plan to celebrate Christmas or attempting to order beef in an Indian restaurant. My most awkward moments have occurred during small talk. *Have I mentioned how much I hate small talk?* Each time I make a mistake, I remind myself to think twice before I speak. But none of those experiences compare to the discomfort of listening to the pain of individuals who live as minorities in predominantly white cultures.

Creating an equitable and just society necessitates the collective engagement of everyone, ranging from casual conversations in our coffee shops to formal debates in the halls of Congress. The absence of a structured national dialogue must not deter us from fostering open and sincere discussions within our circles of family, friends, neighbors, and fellow congregants. By recognizing shared values and collaborating with empathy and respect, we can identify constructive solutions to address historical injustices that have contributed to our racial divides. The path toward healing requires our united effort, a commitment to understanding, and an unwavering dedication to building bridges where barriers once stood.

Jesus exemplified this approach in his interaction with the Samaritan woman by starting the conversation on a level greater than their historical divisions. He met her at the point of her personal experiences, and through this meaningful connection, he was able to speak to broader issues and eventually introduce the hope of the gospel to her. This serves as a model for how to navigate complex conversations in a way that wins hearts and minds.

Jesus' interaction with the Samaritan woman stands as a profound exemple of how we can navigate the intricate landscape of historical divisions, discrimination, and personal experiences. Jesus, instead of allowing their differences to become barriers, met her with empathy and understanding right at the core of her emotional vulnerability. Through this compassionate engagement, he transcended a surface-level conversation to address broader historical and societal realities, ultimately introducing her to the hope of the gospel. This remarkable exchange is a model of conducting complex conversations with grace and wisdom. By recognizing and embracing each other's experiences, seeking shared understanding, and striving for common ground, we lay the foundation for healing, reconciliation, and unity within our communities.

chapter 9

the biltmore princess

extending dignity to those without place

The woman said, "I know that Messiah"
(called Christ) "is coming. When he comes,
he will explain everything to us." Then
Jesus declared, "I, the one speaking to
you—I am he."
—John 4:25–26

Judith and I have a neighbor named Mia. From a distance, she exudes a sense of elegance, carrying herself with a posture that suggests a life of refinement and dignity. Her presence demands your attention and respect. But as you draw closer to her, a different picture comes into focus. Her hair, once lustrous, has become matted; her skin, instead of glowing, is marked by the harsh sun; and her lips, which once might have featured the most expensive lipstick, are now painfully cracked. These contrasts between appearance and reality hint at a life more complex and challenging than it might seem at first glance.

Mia is homeless.

She lives on the streets in our neighborhood.

I can only imagine what happened in her life to create the kind of trauma that makes her more comfortable living on the street than indoors. Judith and I have invited her in, tried to connect her with community resources, and even offered to put her up in a hotel, but she politely refuses in the sweetest of voices.

In the face of her refusal, we feel a little helpless. We pass by her a few times each day as we are coming and going, and we consistently pray for her. Judith calls her the "Biltmore Princess" and prays for her as if she is a member of our own family. Recently, Judith spent a few minutes on the sidewalk trying to convince Mia of her worth and value. She affirmed her beauty, sympathized with her plight, and offered her our assistance. And, once again, Mia declined. But when Judith looked back to wave goodbye, for the first time Mia had her head bowed and appeared to be wiping tears from her eyes.

Mother Teresa once said, "The greatest disease in the West today is not TB or leprosy; it is being unwanted, unloved, and uncared for. We can cure physical diseases with medicine, but the only cure for loneliness, despair, and hopelessness is love."[1] This profound observation serves to remind us that human connection has the power to heal not only the body but also our deepest emotional places.

We've often wondered whether Mia is the reason God led us to sell our home in the suburbs and move to the heart of the city. While it's impossible to know for sure, such a move would be wholly justified if that was the reason. What is abundantly clear, however, is that our world is teeming with souls like Mia. Daily, we cross paths with individuals who, though perhaps not physically homeless, are bereft of a safe space either relationally or emotionally. These encounters invite us to look beyond ourselves, recognizing the unseen needs around us, and to respond with empathy and insight.

Our interactions with Mia are a daily reminder of the importance of seeing those who are homeless as our neighbors. Though they may not have a physical address, a shelter from the sun and rain, and the creature comforts many of us enjoy, they share the same sense of *place* that we do. Some of those who are homeless in my neighborhood have invested as much time and energy into choosing where they live as my wife and I did. In some cases, perhaps even more. Their choice of neighborhoods, street corners, and even which overpass they sleep under is a matter of life and death *every single night*.

The crisis of homelessness has grown steadily during the past thirty years, with almost six hundred million people experiencing homelessness in the United States on any given night. Of these individuals, a significant portion, roughly one-third, are sleeping on the streets, while the remaining two-thirds are in shelters.

Just sit with that sobering statistic for a moment.

If you were to bring together all individuals facing homelessness into a single community, it would have a population comparable to that of Denver, Colorado. The causes of homelessness are multifaceted and deeply rooted in a variety of social, economic, and personal factors. They range from systemic issues like income inequality, lack of affordable housing, and gaps in social safety nets, to more individualized factors like mental-health struggles, substance abuse, and family breakdowns. Employment instability and educational barriers further compound the problem, making it challenging for those affected to break the cycle. Additional layers of complexity emerge when we consider that certain groups, such as minorities, veterans, victims of domestic abuse, LGBTQIA+ youth, and individuals with mental-health conditions, face homelessness at a disproportionately higher rate. For example, African Americans, who make up only 13 percent of the general population, comprise 40 percent of the homeless population, and Indigenous communities experience even higher rates of homelessness. Thus, to effectively address this issue, we must engage in a comprehensive strategy that confronts both systemic and individual causes, while also recognizing that homelessness is fundamentally tied to poverty.

In my own city, the number of homeless individuals has risen dramatically in recent years, with estimates indicating that more than ten thousand men, women, and children reside on our streets. Some are visible, staying in tent cities, under bridges, or in public parks. Others hide in derelict buildings, abandoned cars, or even live in their automobiles, driving nightly from one shopping center to the next to escape being ticketed. Some sleep on our church campuses and bathe in our outdoor baptisteries. Homelessness is a local issue, not an abstract one. Those who live on our streets are not faceless statistics but members of our communities. The largest homeless camp in the country is located a few blocks from our downtown campus; it serves as a microcosm of human misery. This location, known as "The Zone," close to the Central Arizona Shelter Services (CASS) Human Services Campus, has become ground zero for persons experiencing homelessness. The Zone, which is in a busy neighborhood with government offices, historic churches, a funeral-supply shop, and several factories, serves as a visible reminder of the federal and state failure to provide safety for those struggling with addiction, mental illness, and poverty. The call to compassion knows no borders, in both the largest camps and the most remote locations.

Unlike some of my neighbors, not every homeless person lives on the street. Many are couch-surfing in the homes of friends and relatives or shuttled from one shelter to another each night.

Moved by the plight of vulnerable women and children in the community, a city council member from our congregation devised a plan for churches to transform their classrooms into safe spaces for persons experiencing homelessness and to share them on a rotational basis. Our church becomes one of those shelters every other week as our chapel and various classrooms are transformed into the iShelter dormitory for battered women and children. Additionally, for one week each month, our Family Life Center serves as a Family Promise Shelter for displaced families with children. To offer shelter is not merely to provide a roof but to extend a hand of dignity, support, and love. Every chapel and classroom turned dormitory is a sanctuary dedicated to their flourishing.

In recent years, many churches have struggled to address homelessness in their communities, focusing solely on evangelism rather than caregiving. This approach can be confrontational and harmful to those who are traumatized—living in fight or flight mode. By shifting our focus toward caregiving and building relationships based on trust and support, we can offer practical assistance that meets the needs of the homeless and helps them to feel seen and valued. Our faith compels us to see not "the homeless" but our neighbors, our brothers and sisters, struggling right outside our door.[2] Recognition is the first step toward compassionate engagement.

Seeing human suffering is not enough; we must allow ourselves to *feel* it, to truly understand the weight of another's pain. In that connection, born of empathy and compassion, lies the potential for a response rooted in genuine love and understanding. It's all too easy to look upon suffering and remain detached, a stance that can unintentionally dehumanize those in need. But when we open our hearts to see and feel the struggles of others, we can make a profound impact, forging paths toward healing, reconciliation, and true community within our neighborhoods and cities.

A Deeper Question

A half century before my grandparents established their own Shelter Care home for vulnerable persons, Congregationalist pastor Charles Sheldon wrote his classic work depicting the responsibility of Christians toward others in need. *In His Steps: What Would Jesus Do?* was first conceived as a series of narrative sermons delivered to his small congregation in Topeka, Kansas. An advocate for the social gospel, Sheldon wanted to emphasize the responsibility of every church member to love and serve people in need, and his broadest platform was his Sunday-evening pulpit. The sermons began with the story of a homeless man addressing a church about its lack of Christlike mercy. Each week, Sheldon shared another chapter in the unfolding series, posing the question "What would Jesus do?" when his characters faced a moral dilemma.

The idea was so intriguing that his little sanctuary was packed with a spellbound audience each week. At the conclusion of the series, the Chicago *Advance* published Sheldon's sermons as a weekly serial. Afterward, they compiled the chapters and offered them as a ten-cent paperback edition. Since its original publication in 1896, *In His Steps: What Would Jesus Do?* has sold more than fifty million copies, making it one of the bestselling books of all time.

The provocative question Charles Sheldon asked his audience experienced a resurgence a century later when a youth pastor abbreviated it and placed it on a bracelet. Since then, WWJD has been seen on everything from T-shirts to tattoos and from red carpets to major sporting events. Some of my trendiest fashion statements in my midthirties featured a WWJD bracelet with a leather strap and silver snap. One simple bracelet and I was on the fashion runway of evangelism! As dated as the illustration is, Sheldon's premise is worth considering in every generation. No one can deny the transformation that would occur in every community if we would all ask ourselves that question and behave accordingly in every situation. There is, however, a prior question that needs to be asked and answered: Who would Jesus love?

In a world where love is easily extended to the pretty, the powerful, and the popular—all those we aspire to be like—we reluctantly give our compassion to the unlovely, the infirm, and the unimportant. Unfortunately, this form of love leans more toward self-love than the selfless love Jesus manifests toward humanity. Selfless love transcends the boundaries of conditional affection and defies the notion that love is a *quid-pro-quo* exchange. Instead, it embraces an unwavering, unyielding commitment to sacrifice that reaches into the bleakest and most disheartening corners of our lives and the lives of others. This love is also a call to action, urging us to step courageously from the shadows to address the plight of those in our communities who are without safe harbor. It transcends petty differences, uniting us in a common cause that surpasses self-interest and puts the needs of others first. This kind of love embodies the very best of what it is to be human, kind, and compassionate by providing assistance, hope, and healing. Jesus can be seen reaching out to the impoverished and marginalized in the Gospels, extending his hands and heart to them. He described his mission at the beginning of his ministry in the Nazareth synagogue, and it was filled with divine movement: to serve the poor, release prisoners, heal the blind, and break the bonds of injustice.[3] After four hundred years of silence in Israel, he declared that God had spoken and that there was no going back.[4] His message was bursting with life and energy, and he matched his words with actions.

John Mayer brings together ink and melody, forming a

lyric that sticks in the soul: Love is a verb. Love is not a still portrait to be admired from afar but a living, breathing, masterpiece in motion. Love is not content to be an idle longing or a fleeting desire; it has hands that reach, feet that move, and a heart that beats in rhythm with joy and misery. It's a song that sings itself into the lives of others, a refrain that demands our attention and our response. Because love *is,* love *does.*

Somehow, despite the refrain we've heard a thousand times, Jesus' followers often lose sight of this core melody in the gospel. We romanticize the notion that had we danced in Jesus' day, we would have gathered the Samaritans in our warm embrace. Yet we fail to recognize and embrace the Samaritans among us today.

How often do we sit in our cars and blankly stare at the Samaritan standing on the corner?

We see the crude cardboard sign, the grime, the desperation, but we don't see someone's son or daughter, a fellow image-bearer, a possible sibling in Christ, born with the same potential and hopes and dreams as we have. If we see them at all, we turn our heads away, feeling awkward about their request and our inability or unwillingness to respond.

I remember the first time I saw one of those commercials on television representing a humanitarian organization dedicated to feeding starving children in developing countries. You've probably seen them too. Heartbreaking images of malnourished children covered in flies. Toddlers scraping at the sides of empty cans for the smallest scrap of food. Little girls in need of medical care peering out from the door of small, dark shacks. The first time I saw one of those commercials, it broke my heart. I felt an overwhelming, all-consuming sense of compassion for those kids and an intense desire to do something. But then . . .

You know what's coming next, don't you?

As those commercials continued to play day after day, month after month, year after year, they slowly stopped affecting me. Eventually, I became desensitized to their emotional impact, and I found myself changing the channel because I was tired of seeing them. That's the greater tragedy. Psychologically, it's much easier to look past people than to bear witness to their suffering without being able to intervene. When we lack, or perceive that we lack, sufficient resources to meet the needs of others, we reduce them to objects we pass every day, like the bus stop, the bicycle rack, the stop sign. And we change the channel in our minds.

We may have the luxury of turning the channel on poverty because of our own daily needs, but there are 821 million people in the world who are chronically undernourished, and they cannot change the channel and conjure a better life.[5] And millions more can't change the channel on poverty, homelessness, addiction, mental illness, or a hundred other equally devastating experiences.

Hardening our hearts is the way we often manage the circumstances in life that we don't know how to resolve. The news cycle fills our screens, our social-media feeds, and our minds with images of war-torn cities, stories of exploited people, and footage of women and children in deep poverty. All of these human tragedies compete daily for an equal place in the deepest part of our emotions—our compassion.

A hardened heart is often related to a scarcity mindset.

Empathy and Compassion

Early in my pastoral life, I embraced some fundamental misconceptions about empathy and compassion. I observed strong leaders in large congregations and wrongly concluded that emotional guardedness was their key to strength and that investing in a *few* people would prevent me from caring for *many* people. As the years unfolded, I came to a profound realization that not only broadened my understanding but expanded my pastoral vision: expressing empathy for a few people doesn't diminish us; it enriches our hearts and minds, thereby creating a greater capacity to connect with many people. The bigger issue is not how many people I have empathy for; it is how I am ordering my time, talent, and treasure to help them, and that is the function of compassion.

Empathy and compassion, while interconnected, are distinct, both emotionally and spiritually. Empathy relates to how we identify with others in their pain, whereas compassion relates to what we *do* about their pain.

In their groundbreaking work, *Compassionate Leadership: How to Do Hard Things in a Human Way,* Rasmus Hougaard and Jacqueline Carter share the research findings of Tania Singer, one of the world's foremost authorities on empathy and compassion. Through brain imaging, Singer has been able to identify the areas which are activated when we are exposed to suffering.[6] Exposure to suffering registers in the same area of the brain, and in the same manner, as physical pain. Thus, empathy is the ability to *feel* what another person is experiencing, and it is a critical part of our hardwiring as human beings. Empathy allows us to connect with others in their distress emotionally.

For the past decade, empathy has been extolled as a necessary virtue in human interactions, and organizations have worked to disciple their labor force in the art of feeling. Studies have shown that individuals with strong empathy experience greater emotional intelligence, personal contentment, and self-worth. Empathetic people tend to foster broader and more fulfilling social connections, are more actively involved in volunteering, contribute generously to charitable organizations, and readily reach out to assist others in need.[7] This is true of Christians and non-Christians alike. An empathetic world would be a better place for all of us to live in.

But as important as empathy is, it is not enough.

This is where compassion becomes necessary.

Hougaard and Carter argue that compassion goes beyond empathy by not just feeling another's pain but also taking steps to alleviate their suffering. This is a perspective shared by Jeff Weiner, the former CEO of LinkedIn, who is quoted in their book as saying, "Empathy is to see someone suffering under the weight of a great burden and respond by putting the same burden on yourself. Compassion is the act of alleviating the person from the burden."[8] The distinction between empathy and compassion is not semantics; it's a substantial shift from thinking about someone in distress to actually moving toward them.

If empathy is the awareness of human suffering, compassion is its active companion in the trenches, rushing to their aid, coming alongside them, serving them in their distress.

The word *compassion* is one of the strangest words you

will read in the New Testament. The Greek verb is *splagchnizomai*, and it relates to our inner organs—intestines, kidneys, liver, and even bowels.[9] The Hebrew counterpart is frequently used in the Old Testament to describe God's heart toward the poor and the powerless, but *splagchnizomai* appears only a dozen times in the New Testament. To be moved with compassion means to be provoked in the deepest part of your inner being. To the early Greeks, human emotions were thought to exist in the gut; we still describe feeling fear or dread in the pit of the stomach. Compassion is not an intellectual response, or even an emotional or sentimental response. It is visceral—something felt deep inside, at our core, and it cannot be ignored.

Throughout the Gospels we see Jesus moved by the sight of both individuals and multitudes who were hungry, grieving, lost, sick, or in some other need.[10] Not only did he bear witness to their suffering, but he internalized their pain and it drove him to action. The sight of human suffering in its worst forms is heart-wrenching, but it is even more devastating to witness it and not respond. Jesus teaches us that bearing witness to the suffering of others is not enough—we must take action to alleviate it.

When Jesus told the story of the good Samaritan, he used that same word, *splagchnizomai*, to describe the way the Samaritan was moved with compassion for the man who had been beaten and robbed. With the use of this phrase, Jesus was describing the deep inward movement of a stranger toward a suffering Jew. He was connecting the Samaritan to himself and the empathy he felt for people in pain.

Compassion is the act of being kind and understanding

to others, knowing that they, too, are human beings who suffer. You do not have to give up your job to work in a homeless shelter. It might appear in simple actions such as offering a seat to a pregnant woman, being polite to service employees, assisting a friend with a move, or taking the time to listen to a colleague. These small gestures may appear to be insignificant, yet they may make a tremendous difference in someone's day and even prevent feelings of burnout for both the giver and the recipient.

Corridors and Rooms

Life's journey takes us through corridors and rooms filled with encounters and experiences; we brush past some individuals and linger with others. Jesus demonstrated profound discernment in this dance, recognizing when to pause and when to continue on his path. He regularly stopped to heed those in need, no matter their social rank or supposed insignificance, aligning his actions with the divine will of his heavenly Father. His disciples often urged him to overlook the afflicted and move on, yet Jesus chose to extend his reach, his arms open wide, his heart receptive.

Jesus' unwavering dedication to serving others is beautifully portrayed in his interactions with the beggar, the children, the hemorrhaging woman, and Zacchaeus. Through these interactions, he taught us that no soul is too humble to warrant his attention, no person unworthy of his healing embrace. He paused to grasp their fears, engage with their struggles, and comfort their grief, becoming a witness to their human condition.

We all need someone to bear witness to our suffering, even when they lack the resources to change our situation.

When Jesus met the Samaritan woman, he saw beyond the social stigma and prejudices associated with her and recognized her as a human being created in the image of God, deserving of love and respect. He engaged her in a meaningful conversation, and through their time together she came to understand more about the nature of God and the truth of the Messiah. His choice to reveal himself as the Messiah to this unnamed woman on the fringes of society, rather than to the rich and powerful, highlights how he sees and values humanity.

In traveling to more than sixty countries, I have seen pain and suffering on a widespread scale. I've visited the garbage dumps in Mexico City, where a woman begged my wife to take her baby because she couldn't feed her any longer. I've wept tears in the favelas of Rio de Janeiro as I bore witness to hopelessness and despair among the impoverished. I've held dying AIDS babies in the shadow cities in Africa, such as Khayelitsha, where one million people live in squalor. And I've lead humanitarian teams to places like Port-au-Prince, Haiti, after a massive earthquake ripped open the floor of the city, leaving three hundred thousand dead and another three hundred thousand injured.

And in all of those places, I've left people suffering on the streets to return to the comfort of my own family, my own home, and my own financial well-being. It breaks my heart to leave suffering people in their circumstances without alleviating their distress. There are moments when it feels like the world is worsening despite our modern technological advances. I've had those days when I wonder, "Am I making any difference for anyone, anywhere in the world?" Perhaps you've had them too. It keeps us reaching, serving, working for the common good of all people.

The magnitude of poverty and suffering in the world can be overwhelming, leading to feelings of helplessness and the temptation to turn away. In a country like the United States, where resources are readily available, we can respond to the 37.25 million individuals living in poverty, the 400,000 children in foster care, and the more than 2 million people incarcerated.

In the face of such suffering, it can be easy to shut ourselves off, insulate ourselves with comfort, and ignore the reality around us. It is crucial to remember that empathy and compassion are where the journey to making a difference begins. We must allow ourselves to feel the pain of others before we can come alongside them to help. Otherwise, people like me are in danger of becoming weekend warriors, virtue signalers, white saviors. We already have a Savior, and he shows us what it means to serve others.

In Jesus' encounter with the Samaritan woman, we find a model for interaction that begins with a humble human connection. Engaging with our neighbors, even those we encounter on the streets, can start with something as simple as asking their names and inviting them to share their stories. This small act can open a gateway to forming relationships, enabling us to discern how best to serve them. Service may take the form of prayer, sharing a meal, extending an invitation into a safe space, connecting them with resources, or simply promising a return visit. Loving others is not a one-size-fits-all endeavor; each person requires a unique approach. But by initiating conversations with compassion and recognizing their individuality, we can positively impact their lives.

Compassion is a lot like jazz: fluid, unscripted, full of movement, bursting with energy, carrying us along the twists and turns of life. And for some people that may feel like a scary and unpredictable way to live. Living in the flow—embracing the unexpected, the serendipitous connections, and the opportunities to make a real difference in someone's life—infuses our existence with purpose and joy.

I wouldn't want to live any other way.

Radical Acceptance

In the center of a small Belgian town sits a church dedicated to Saint Dymphna, a seventh-century woman who dedicated her life to serving the mentally disabled. For more than seven hundred years, the residents of Geel, Belgium, have followed her example of selfless service by accepting people with mental disorders into their homes to care for them.

A nineteenth-century psychiatrist noted that, in Geel, "treating the insane meant to simply live with them, share their work, their distractions" and that this treatment kept them from losing "their dignity as reasonable human beings."[11]

As this custom has evolved, it has become more formalized with psychiatric treatments and funding from the government. But at the heart of the program remains the practice of radical acceptance as people are welcomed in just as they are. It's seen in the language: the people are called boarders instead of patients, and they're never identified by their diseases. The families who take them in are not even told their diagnoses. This blurs the lines between patients and caregivers, boarders and nonboarders, and those with and without mental illness. When those lines blur, people are simply treated as people and differences are easier to accept.

A recent evaluation of the program noted that the "acceptance of mental differences has become something of a tradition in Geel. It's at the heart of the boarder program, and some observers think it's also responsible for the system's success."[12]

It's not hard to imagine what would happen to those boarders if they weren't welcomed into people's homes. In the US, 40 percent of people living on the streets and more than 50 percent of people in prison have a mental health disorder.[13] If they aren't welcomed in, then they are cast out, left to deal with their pain alone.

Life is a messy, painful experience for most of us, even for people of faith. We suffer in every way because of the brokenness of our world, and so does everyone around us. To paraphrase Ian Maclaren, "Be kind, for everyone you meet is engaged in the fight of their life."

In recent years, the prevalence of mental illness in the United States has risen significantly, with one in four individuals experiencing a mental health disorder.[14] Anxiety disorders, in particular, are a major concern, with more than forty million Americans experiencing panic attacks or anxiety disorders each year.[15] The US has consistently appeared at the top of every global survey on anxiety over the past two decades.[16]

The use of medication to treat anxiety and the impact of stress-related issues on medical care and productivity is staggering, with estimates placing the cost at $300 billion annually.[17] A renowned psychologist has noted that the average child in the United States today experiences the same level of stress and anxiety as the average psychiatric patient in the 1950s.[18]

How are we to respond to these overwhelming conditions? *Ministry with Persons with Mental Illness and their Families* was written to answer that question. At the risk of oversimplification, the authors conclude that people with mental illness "are not so much looking for answers as they are looking for understanding."[19] This understanding is described as a form of radical acceptance, where simply being present and warm with the person or family can make a difference.[20]

Radical acceptance is not the goal but the foundation upon which we can build transformative relationships. It's an essential starting point that, by embracing others, opens both parties to the unique comfort and healing that only God can provide.

The promise of solace, in the raw and painful turmoil of life, is conveyed all through the Scriptures. God is referred to be "the Father of mercies and God of all comfort, who comforts us in all our tribulation."[21] The work of the Holy Spirit is also marked by comfort and counsel. The Holy Spirit, described as the *Parakletos* in Greek—a name that means advocate, helper, or comforter—is to walk alongside us, supplying assistance in our times of need.[22] This relationship improves our ability to connect with people and reflects God's desire for compassion and empathy in our communities.

It was only after establishing a human connection with her that he revealed his identity as the Messiah.

The words of the Samaritan woman resonate with our deepest hopes and longings: "I know that Messiah is coming."[23] The unsaid part is what we long for most: *And when he arrives, he will set the wrongs of the world right.* As believers, we know the end of the story, that Jesus will return to restore a broken world. But we are left with lingering questions: How do we manage until he arrives? What do we do between the pain and the promise? How do we endure another painful bout with depression? How do we live through another messy breakup? How do we pay the bills? How do we keep our marriages together and our families intact?

And how do we help those who are suffering on the streets of our cities?

The Samaritan woman was looking for the Messiah in the maze of rules and religion, never imagining that he would meet her in her own daily experience, in the middle of her brokenness and shame. And yet that is where the Savior is always found. He sits with the meek and lowly, not the arrogant and wealthy.

Many people view the church today as unapproachable and disconnected from the problems of everyday life. They see the church as an institution that is more concerned with its own agenda rather than a source of compassion and understanding for those who are struggling. As a result, many people who do not have a connection to the church often feel that it is not a place where they can find the support and understanding they need.

Recent studies have shown that, in order to bridge this gap

between the unchurched and the church, we must first focus on building a connection with them based on Jesus' humanity before they will ever accept his divinity. This means high-lighting the fact that Jesus was a real person who lived in the world and understood the struggles and hardships we face. When people see that Jesus was a human being who cared deeply about the needs of others, they are more likely to see the church as a place that can provide them with the support and care they need.

A compassionate church is the answer to a hurting world.

chapter 10

neighborhood watch

relational dynamics and
conflict resolution

Just then his disciples returned and were
surprised to find him talking with a woman.
But no one asked, "What do you want?" or
"Why are you talking with her?" Then, leaving
her water jar, the woman went back to the
town and said to the people, "Come, see a
man who told me everything I ever did. Could
this be the Messiah?" They came out of the
town and made their way toward him.

—John 4:27–30

My middle son and his wife reside in Phoenix's Willo historic district, one of the city's earliest master-planned communities dating back to the 1920s. This vibrant neighborhood exudes a unique blend of architectural styles, including Tudors, bungalows, Spanish colonials, and early ranch homes, all meticulously constructed along palm-lined streets. The community's pride of ownership is unmistakable, and their annual home tour draws thousands of eager visitors who wait in line for hours to explore the area's quaint little homes. Beyond its charming, picturesque houses, this neighborhood is renowned for its robust sense of community. Neighbors not only know each other but also offer genuine support. Children freely play across adjoining yards, while adults exchange friendly waves from their front porches. There's an undeniable sense of mutual care and concern here. My son and his wife have found great joy in being part of such a tight-knit community.

I love visiting their little neighborhood, but there's one thing that bothers me. The residents have strategically posted dozens of signs throughout the neighborhood that ominously read: Neighborhood Watch. The white poster depicts the black silhouette of a burglar, dressed like a detective from the 1920s, with a red strike-through.

The message is clear.

We are watching you.

Especially if you dress like Dick Tracy.

Have you ever driven through a community with those neighborhood-watch signs? What's the first thing that goes through your mind? Those two words always inspire a lot of paranoia as I wonder, "Who is watching?" "Where are they watching from?" "Are they watching me right *now?*" And all of that usually leads me to wonder: "What happened in this neighborhood that was so bad that they have to have people watching?"

One little sign can send some major messages. On the positive side, it sends a message about caring for others: "We care about those who live on this block. We see our neighbors as friends and want to protect them from harm. We are here to look after one another." On the negative side, it sends a message about fearing the other. It says, "You aren't from this neighborhood. We don't know you, and you don't belong here."

Both of those messages are bound up in this human experience. We all long to be a part of a caring community with our best interests at heart, yet we have learned to fear the other because, let's be honest, a lot has gone down in the neighborhood.

From Adam and Eve outside the garden to today, human history is full of stories of anger, violence, robbery, and every kind of sin in every type of neighborhood. Our best efforts to create harmonious communities buckle beneath the weight of our self-centeredness. And even if people in one neighborhood manage to care reasonably well for each other, there's always another neighborhood that everyone knows to avoid.

Maybe that's how Jesus' disciples felt in this story as they entered what was historically known as a dangerous neighborhood with a painful history. When they saw Jesus engaged in a conversation with the Samaritan woman, they must have gone on the defensive, wondering about her motives and why Jesus was entertaining them.

The disciples knew the long history of conflict between

Jews and Samaritans and the checkered history of Shechem. They would have been aware of the story of Dinah's rape and how her father ignored her abuse and tried to commoditize it. They knew the history of Joseph being attacked by his own brothers and sold into slavery there. And they had no interest in hanging around that neighborhood.

Jesus didn't share his disciples' apprehension. Instead, he entered the painful legacy of Shechem as one who had come to redeem and restore the broken places in our world and those who dwell in them. To Jesus, Shechem wasn't a neighborhood to avoid but another place to extend his love and compassion. There was no community support when Dinah and Joseph suffered there, but Jesus had come to watch over it in a way that does more than bear witness to injustice—he had come to heal it.

Every church is called to be the neighborhood watch in their community, caring for people in need and creating safe spaces for all who dwell there. This isn't an easy mission in a fractured and fractious world. It requires humility, curiosity, empathy, a willingness to listen and learn, and the courage to identify with the pain of a community in a way that says, "I'm not here as your savior but as a fellow sufferer. And along with you, I'm searching for a better way." Having a passport into neighborhoods is based on our willingness to become humble, teachable, and even vulnerable.

East of Eden

The pain that went down in the very first neighborhood still lives with us today. The garden of Eden was meant to be a safe place for humanity to live in harmony with all creation, but when Adam and Eve disobeyed, they were banished from utopia. They moved east of Eden, carrying the invisible and deadly sin virus into their new community. Things seemed to go well in their new neighborhood for a while, at least as well as they can when you're living in exile. But, before long, sin manifested its destructive force, and the neighborhood exploded in violence.

Violence.

There is no hint or mention of it for the first few decades of our existence.

And when it explodes all over the pages of the Bible, it is in the context of a family.

There were two brothers born of Adam and Eve: Cain, a cultivator of the earth, and Abel, a tender of flocks. Both brought an offering to the Lord when it came time for the harvest. While Cain brought *some* of his crops, Abel brought the best portions of the firstborns of his flock. Cain's offering was perennial and would regrow the following season, making it less than genuinely sacrificial. Abel's offering was costly and irreplaceable. The Lord, in his wisdom, accepted Abel's offering but not Cain's, and this rejection sparked a fire of jealousy and rage within Cain. The Lord spoke to him, reminding him that his offering would have been accepted if he had acted justly. Even more, the Lord warned him of what was to come, saying, "Sin is crouching at your door; it desires to have you, but you must rule over it."[1]

Instead of taking the Lord's advice to heart, Cain took his brother's life. It seems like an incomprehensible reaction, doesn't it? But that's what happens when we perceive the other as objects responsible for our feelings, emotions, and experiences. When we make others accountable for our emotional states and they fail to live up to our expectations, the natural recourse is to remove them from our lives in one way or another. Following Abel's murder, the Lord confronted Cain, inquiring about his brother's whereabouts. Instead of confessing and repenting, Cain retorted, "I don't know. . . . Am I my brother's keeper?"[2]

The narrative in this story makes me wonder how Cain could be oblivious to the Lord's omniscience. Was his heart so hardened and calloused that he just didn't care? His behavior may have been as much an act of defiance against the Lord as it was a retaliation against his brother.

The story of Cain and Abel serves as a poignant reminder of the devastating impact of human conflict. This tale of sibling rivalry was the first sign of what was to come, the ongoing battle among brothers, tribes, nations, and even people of faith. Significantly, this tragedy occurred soon after the fall of man, underscoring the inescapable consequences of Adam and Eve's sin. Their bitter legacy, still in its infancy, had already affected the next generation. The inevitability of Abel's death is almost palpable, adding to the despair of the story.

The effects of sin are amplified with each new generation. Though Cain is Adam's firstborn son, his character and behavior are strikingly different. Adam is responsible for exercising dominion over animals, while Cain desires to control other humans. Adam is ashamed of his sin and confesses it, while Cain denies his wrongdoing with defiance. Adam accepts his punishment willingly, but Cain argues and appeals.

These contrasting actions of father and son reveal the

exponential growth of sin and its consequences from one generation to the next. It warns us how quickly evil can spread, leading to violence and destruction. Cain's defiance and denial are a testament to the all-consuming power of sin and how it blinds us to the truth. The one thing they hold in common is that both were deserving of death for their disobedience.

This first murder is a reminder of the fragility of familial bonds, and those who have experienced conflict with siblings will testify to the emotional toll it takes. Losing a relationship with a family member can be akin to losing a limb, where one still instinctively reaches out in moments of joy or sorrow only to be reminded that the connection has been severed. I know what that feels like.

For three decades, I was estranged from my younger brother; thankfully, that painful season is now behind. In recent discussions, we both agree that, despite the pressures of growing up in a pastor's home, our childhood seemed quite ordinary, a picture of the ups and downs of a family. Like all other siblings, we quarreled, made amends, played together, and behaved as kids generally do. As we navigated through adolescence and into our teenage years, the three-year age gap naturally led us to form our own circles of friends. I went to college early, married, and eventually started my own family. A few years later, Tim came to visit us, and under the pressures of being a young husband, a new father, and a church planter, I said some things in exasperation that I deeply regret.

Tim vanished as quickly as he had appeared on our doorstep.

And for thirty long years we were estranged.

Tim distinguished himself as a highly decorated combat

veteran during those three decades, receiving five Purple Hearts and five Bronze Stars. His journey took him from Iraq's barren deserts to Afghanistan's rugged mountains and beyond to numerous undisclosed locations, his life resembling a tale fit for a novel. The government altered his identity to safeguard our family and limited our interactions to the bare minimum. Every few years, we would receive a brief phone call on special occasions like Thanksgiving or Christmas or during moments that evoked nostalgia for him. This fleeting connection made us hope everything would return to normal. It didn't happen.

After thirty years of alienation, he suddenly reappeared one day. Despite the fact that he was no longer in the military, he chose to keep the persona he had taken for so long. It had become an essential part of his identity. Tim left our house as a teenager to join the US Army's 82nd Airborne Division. And in his place, another appeared, a different man, born of a thirty-year absence.

Family Dynamics

It's a rare family that hasn't experienced some form of "family dynamics," as we euphemistically describe them, especially during the past few years. Though 2020 is well behind us, the pandemic took a toll on many relationships, causing bonds that were already strained to reach their breaking point. The pandemic intensified rifts in countless families, from opposing views on vaccinations to heated debates on mask-wearing to the stress of being cooped up with little respite. And that was on top of the bitter divisions of the previous presidential election cycle. As a result, I pastor parents and grandparents who grieve their losses and wonder if things will ever return to their prepandemic state.

The story of Cain and Abel is interpreted as a tale of sibling rivalry, but it can also be seen as a story about how to relate to the other.

We may perceive members of our family as the other for a variety of reasons. Although we grow up in the same household, united by shared values, over time, our journey takes us into new environments where we encounter new relationships and are exposed to new ideas. When taken to heart, those ideas form new perspectives that further shape our sense of being. This new identity may not fit well within our family of origin and might even be considered a threat to our families' sense of uniqueness and belonging.

In most areas of life, when faced with relationships that refuse to embrace our true selves, we find it easy to distance ourselves from those who reject us. But when it comes to our familial bonds, we are inextricably linked in a manner that cannot be easily broken. So we resist and embrace, draw close and push away.

It's also worth noting that the sense of otherness can be mutual, and the feeling of being the other may go both ways. For example, parents may see their child as the other because of their lifestyle choices, but the child may also perceive their parents as the other because of their values or beliefs.

Regardless of your family dynamics, you've likely asked Cain's question when it comes to other people in your world: "Am I my brother's keeper?" That question strikes at the heart of the human condition, and Cain's response lays bare our way of thinking: "Do I have to be responsible for other people? Can't I just focus on taking care of myself?"

At its core, the Bible is about being one another's keepers.

From the Old Testament, the call to care for our neighbors was not restricted to those within our familial groups or tribal communities. God instructed his people to treat foreigners as respectfully and kindly as they treated their families. Of the Ten Commandments, the first four focus on our relationship with God, and the last six govern our earthly relationships. Fundamentally, they all serve to protect the other. This means honoring them by refraining from murder, adultery, deceit, theft, or false testimony. Our relationship with God is contingent on our relationships with each other.

The call to be a good neighbor is even more apparent in the New Testament. Jesus, in summarizing the Law and the prophets, emphasizes the command to love God and love others as ourselves. The parable of the good Samaritan expands the definition of neighbor to include every human being, even our enemies. It is as if Jesus declared once and for all that we are all responsible for caring for one another as a part of the neighborhood watch.

The apostle Paul was a passionate community builder who had spent the first part of his life behaving much like Cain. Driven by a sense of loyalty to his Jewish faith, he persecuted and murdered his Christian brothers, believing them to be infidels. Yet after encountering God's transformative love on the road to Damascus, his heart softened and he became like Abel. Abandoning the rage that once defined his religious convictions, Paul became a loving, spiritual father to many first-century Christian communities.

Paul was deeply committed to the well-being of the communities he served, familiar with the pain of division, and passionate about maintaining unity. Far from being autocratic, Paul was accommodating, putting the greater good first. He advocated for the inclusion of ethnicities, condemned arbitrary exclusions, and exemplified a balance of encouragement and accountability. His teachings encourage us to be good neighbors by avoiding divisive activities such as gossip and instead offering support and assistance. While he was outspoken in his opposition to incorrect theology and disobedience of apostolic authority, his ultimate goal was church unity. Yet despite Paul's dedication, Jesus' teachings, and countless others advocating for peace and community, the church often falters in embodying basic tenets of faith: love for our neighbors, kindness to strangers, compassion for the needy, and mercy for the sinful.

We haven't done well at "one-anothering" one another.

The human need for love and support amplifies the necessity of cultivating vibrant church communities that serve as microcosms of harmonious neighborhoods. The church can be a luminous example of unity and love in today's fragmented world. Imagine a church aflame with love for God, rich in relationships, and aligned in mission—so captivating that it evokes envy in skeptics, drawing them toward community and faith.

Love should be the inspiration for everything we do, guiding all of our words, deeds, and acts. Without it, our assertions of faith and allegiance to ideology are worthless and hollow. The best demonstration of our belief in the gospel and its life-changing potential is how we treat others, especially those who are unlike us or whom we may find it difficult to love, even within our families.

Neighborhood Dynamics

The story of Cain and Abel is also an archetype of community violence. Their sibling rivalry sets in motion a cycle of violence repeated throughout history in neighborhoods worldwide. When people feel they are being mistreated or their needs are not being met, they lash out at those nearest to their pain. In the story, Cain's jealousy and anger toward Abel escalate until the animosity erupts into physical violence. Similarly, conflicts between individuals or groups may start small in neighborhoods, but they can quickly escalate into more serious violence if not addressed and resolved.

If the church is serious about being a neighborhood watch, we must learn how to resolve community conflict beyond our walls.

In my city, the neighborhoods are like individual tiles in a beautiful mosaic, and I suspect this is true of yours as well. America is experiencing racial and socioeconomic diversification at a rate not seen since the early twentieth century, and our neighborhoods reflect this growing diversity. As a result, each community is unique in its character, culture, and history. It is a microcosm of humanity where we can observe many facets of human life and experience. And it is situated in the larger context of our city.

I see the challenges and triumphs of everyday life played out in these neighborhoods. I see families struggling to make ends meet while others live in abundance. I see vibrant and

diverse communities while others are struggling with poverty and crime. I see people of different races, cultures, and
socioeconomic backgrounds living together, sometimes in
harmony or conflict.

This diversity is both a blessing and a challenge. On the
one hand, it enriches our city with its different perspectives,
cultures, and traditions. But on the other hand, it can create tension and division when people cannot appreciate and
respect each other's differences.

I hope we can learn to appreciate and celebrate our
neighborhoods' diversity and work together to create an inclusive, equitable, and just city. This will require us to learn from
one another, listen, understand, and find common ground.
Only then can we truly embrace the rich tapestry of our city's
neighborhoods and create a better future for all.

In recent years, policymakers have increasingly recognized the potential for faith-based organizations, including
churches, synagogues, and mosques, to contribute to
community-strengthening efforts. This recognition is evident in initiatives like the Charitable Choice provision, which
allows faith-based organizations to compete for government
funding on equal footing with secular organizations for providing social services. By promoting collaboration between
the public sector and faith-based entities, this provision aims
to harness their unique capacities to address social issues and
enhance community well-being.

The optimism surrounding the expanded role of
faith-based organizations stems from a desire to explore
alternative approaches beyond sole reliance on the public sector. Notably, the successes achieved by some large churches

in areas like housing and economic development have set high expectations and demonstrated the potential for faith communities to drive positive change, particularly in under-served neighborhoods. But it is essential to approach these developments thoughtfully, considering complexities such as religious liberty, accountability, and inclusivity. Policymakers, community stakeholders, and churches must navigate these nuances carefully to ensure that collaborations uphold principles of nondiscrimination, respect for diverse perspectives, and inclusivity, without infringing on religious liberties. This ongoing exploration reflects the search for innovative and holistic approaches to address societal challenges and invites continued dialogue and collaboration for the creation of thriving communities.

We can serve as peacemakers and community builders only to the degree that we have allowed peace and communal living to be formed in *us*. According to what Jesus taught, our conflicts emanate from our interior world.[3] They lie deep within us. Violated rights, unmet needs, and unrealistic expectations erupt on the surface in anger, rejection, and division. To resolve these conflicts, we must first face and acknowledge them. It is essential to recognize that the underlying causes are rooted in more profound issues such as fear, loss of control, and lack of trust in God's care and provision.

Violated rights.

Unmet needs.

Unrealistic expectations.

When the disciples returned to find Jesus in a conversation with the Samaritan woman, they were shocked. What they witnessed must have been far beyond the norm because the passage says, "None of them had the nerve to ask, 'What do you want with her?' or 'Why are you talking to her?'"[4] How many times do we see the disciples so unnerved that they can't even muster a question or complaint? Not many. Their distress only intensified when Jesus stayed there, dedicating the next two days to teaching and ministering to the people.

During moments like these, it helps me to remember that the disciples were all in their late teens and early twenties when Jesus called them to follow him. They began like all of us, self-centered and self-absorbed, seeing themselves as the center of the universe. Over time, they became less like their early selves and more like the world-changing leaders we know them as. We see their extraordinary spiritual growth throughout the New Testament.

Had Jesus not been present, it's evident that the situation with the disciples would have played out quite differently. Even after spending two days watching Jesus treat the other with kindness and respect, their ongoing bias against the Samaritans proves how difficult it is to let go of past prejudices, even for disciples of Jesus. Of course, if they were traveling without Jesus, it's more likely that the disciples would have circumvented Samaria altogether. Shunning conflict, however, is not the same as resolving it.

Conflict avoidance is not an effective form of community building.

Conflict resolution is a crucial aspect of community building, as conflicts are a natural and unavoidable part of human interactions. We must remind ourselves that conflict is not necessarily negative, because differences in opinions and perspectives can lead to growth and progress. When conflicts are not addressed healthily and constructively, however, they can escalate and cause division, leading to irreparable damage within communities.

For most of us, our approach toward conflict resolution is nothing like that of the first siblings and more like the disciples'. Instead of resorting to violence, we become quietly judgmental, cynical, and questioning, or passive-aggressive. But these actions still lead to division in our families, communities, and churches. The fruit of the disciples' refusal to accept the Samaritans as the other explodes in the murderous spirit of Cain shortly after this weekend retreat.

It happened on a return trip to Jerusalem near the end of Jesus' life. Jesus was going to allow himself to be taken and crucified as a sacrifice for the sins of humanity. And he had set his face like flint in anticipation of all that was to come. This journey also meant passing by a Samaritan village—one of Jesus' favorite places to visit. Yet surprisingly, the Samaritans did not welcome him into their community.[5]

One of the gospel writers, Luke, highlights that Jesus knew full well that this rejection was part of God's plan for him to reach his appointed destination. He was not taken aback by the hostility but rather viewed it as an opportunity to fulfill God's purpose. Whether knowingly or unknowingly, the Samaritans were helping him stay focused on the task ahead.

Despite all his positive experiences with the Samaritans, Jesus still faced rejection by this one village. Although he had the right to appeal, he chose not to. This is because it was not part of the divine plan for him to be in that village then. Stopping to visit would have delayed his trip to Jerusalem, and it would have interfered with his mission leading to the cross and the salvation of the world. Their rejection worked in concert with his divine mission.

Even in the face of their rejection, Jesus' love and compassion toward the Samaritans showcase his unwavering commitment to their people. He stood in solidarity with them and saw them as worthy of love and respect, despite their troubled past with his people. Jesus' love and kindness toward those who reject him is a testament to his boundless capacity for compassion and empathy.

Not understanding the divine plan, two of Jesus' disciples, James and John, wanted to burn down the village.[6] But Jesus rebuked them and reminded them to recognize the role of the Holy Spirit in their lives. He emphasized that the primary reason for his coming was to save lives, not destroy them. And in the following chapter, when Jesus reacted to the impenitence of certain cities by publicly naming and shaming Chorazin, Bethsaida, Capernaum, Tyre, and Sidon, he didn't mention the Samaritan village, recognizing their rejection as in line with the divine plan for his life and assignment.[7]

It isn't Jesus' nature to fall in and out of love with people. Once he gives his heart, there's no taking it back.

chapter 11

won't you be my neighbor?

love leads us forward

Many of the Samaritans from that town believed in him because of the woman's testimony, "He told me everything I ever did." So when the Samaritans came to him, they urged him to stay with them, and he stayed two days. And because of his words many more became believers. They said to the woman, "We no longer believe just because of what you said; now we have heard for ourselves, and we know that this man really is the Savior of the world."

—John 4:39–42

This past summer Judith and I had our grand-daughter, Alexandria Sophia, with us for two weeks while her parents were on vacation. We planned our summer break at the same time so we could look after Lexi, and since we live in a high-rise building that isn't ideal for a three-year-old, we took her on a trip to Sedona, a picturesque little community just north of Phoenix.

The vacation home we were staying in provided house-keeping every other day, so on the second day we were there, the housekeeping crew rang the doorbell, and I went to answer it. When I opened the door and invited them in, Lexi came running across the living room toward them with her arms wide open and a huge smile on her face, and she said, "Oh, our neighbors are here!" It was an unforgettable moment.

Here was a privileged white child standing before three dear ladies who had come to clean the house, but she didn't see them as the cleaning crew. She saw them for who they were: our neighbors. Judith and I have stayed in this home enough over the past few years to have begun building a relationship with these ladies, but in one single moment Lexi connected with them at a deeper level than we had in a dozen previous conversations.

And it was all because she identified them as our neighbors.

The next eight days were a master class in hospitality. Inspired by Lexi's openness, we increased our efforts to strengthen this bond. On the surface, the dynamics of our relationship were the same—they were still there to do their jobs, and we were still on a working vacation. Yet something profound had shifted, turning the transactional relationship into a more personal one. We learned their names, shared our stories, and began to understand their lives a whole lot better.

In the ensuing months, whenever we visit, they come a little early to chat, stay around a little longer than normal to say goodbye, and recently asked about the worship service we were blasting on YouTube. I've shared the gospel with enough people to identify the signs of God at work in their lives, and the evidence is undeniable with these dear ladies. Their growing curiosity and our deepening relationship testify to the transformative power of hospitality.

In the modern age, we often define hospitality too narrowly, as entertaining friends, throwing a party, or having guests over for dinner. But the biblical idea runs much deeper. Hospitality is a means of inclusion, acceptance, and justice, and it is an expression of holiness. Seeing strangers as neighbors is central to hospitality, as Lexi intuitively understood.

God cares more about hospitality than we could ever imagine. The word "hospitality" in Greek is *philoxenia*, which literally means "love of strangers." It is the opposite of *xenophobia*, or fear of strangers. In ancient Israel, the laws of hospitality meant you were obligated to provide food, shelter, and protection to any strangers who came to your door.[1]

Biblically speaking, hospitality is an invitation to include the other in our communities as one of us, with all the rights and privileges that come with that. It is the act of extending privileges across differences. Hospitality is grace given to friends and strangers. Welcoming, connecting, and even eating together says "we belong to each other" in a profoundly meaningful way.

The rapid expansion of the gospel throughout the Roman

Empire can be attributed, in part, to the distinct form of hospitality practiced by Christians. In ancient Rome, offering hospitality to strangers in need of sustenance or shelter was considered a civic duty. Among familiar individuals, however, hospitality was leveraged as a means of enhancing one's honor. In a culture that placed great emphasis on honor and shame, an individual's initial standing in society was determined by the honor of their family. Consequently, every action and circumstance in life could either increase or diminish one's honor. Committing a crime, contracting a disease, or suffering financial loss could result in a loss of honor, while engaging in successful debates, thriving in business, or being invited to a prestigious dinner party could boost it. Transactional hospitality carried with it an obligation to repay the favor, leading people to extend hospitality only to those who could reciprocate and accept hospitality only from those they could repay in kind.

Jesus defied the cultural norms of transactional hospitality and encouraged his followers to do the same.[2] Unlike others who upheld these norms, he welcomed all to his table, whether they were tax collectors or Pharisees, sinful or virtuous, or labeled any other way. He never expected anything in return for his acts of kindness. Instead he taught his disciples to offer hospitality to those who were unable to repay it.[3] He extended an invitation to belong to his community to all whom he encountered, disregarding their social status and reputation. Jesus not only reached out to the marginalized, the needy, and the outcasts, but he also instructed his disciples to seek them out and invite them to partake in the feast.[4]

The early followers of Jesus emulated his example, rejecting the transactional norms of hospitality. The apostles opposed the notion of favoring people of higher standing in their communities.[5] They opened their homes and their tables to all, freely sharing their resources so that no one among them was in need.[6] This spirit of generosity and love was a defining characteristic of the early church, and it earned them a reputation for compassion.

They treated outsiders as though they were members of their own families. Christian hospitality stands in stark contrast to the hospitality of the world and even to modern-day norms. It involves extending the boundless grace of God's kingdom to people in need, going beyond merely inviting people to join us in our activities. True hospitality entails integrating individuals into our lives, accepting them as insiders who belong to our communities, even before they embrace the faith.

The essence of Christian hospitality is breaking down the walls of separation between people, transcending the distinctions between "insiders" and "outsiders," "members" and "nonmembers," and offering everyone a place of belonging.

Regrettably, the approach to hospitality has undergone a major shift from the early days of Christianity to modern times. Instead of demonstrating countercultural hospitality, we now expect people to conform to certain beliefs and behaviors before granting them a place in our church communities. This goes against the example set by Jesus, who welcomed those who were far from God into his community with open arms and unconditional love, long before they ever believed in him.

Radical hospitality, which serves as the foundation of the Christian experience and ministry, has been a defining characteristic of believers who have faithfully served God throughout history. It is an expression of God's nature displayed toward the world.

In contrast to the distant and demanding gods of ancient times, our God is a hospitable deity, opening his heart and his home to us. We see this aspect of his character throughout the story of the Bible.

Let's look deeper at just two examples. God's hospitality is beautifully depicted in the creation of the garden of Eden and the placement of humanity within its lush, abundant embrace. In Genesis, we witness God's intentional design and meticulous care in crafting a perfect dwelling place for his beloved creation. Every detail, from the flourishing vegetation to the flowing rivers, was carefully fashioned with humanity in mind. God's act of creating a garden of unimaginable beauty and abundance reflects his deep desire to provide a nurturing and hospitable environment for his beloved children. In this sacred space, God welcomed Adam and Eve, inviting them to partake freely of the bountiful offerings of the garden, providing for their every need. The garden of Eden stands as a testament to God's unwavering hospitality, as he extended the fullness of his love, provision, and care to humanity. It exemplifies the essence of hospitality—a generous and gracious welcome into a place of safety, nourishment, and belonging. Through the creation of the garden of Eden, God set the stage for a profound relationship with humanity, demonstrating his desire to create a home filled with love, harmony, and unending hospitality.

Abraham, known as the father of our faith, stands as an early example of the gospel through his remarkable embodiment of hospitality. In Genesis, we see Abraham's unwavering commitment to welcome strangers with open arms.[7] When three men appeared near his tent, he immediately recognized the divine presence among them and extended an extravagant display of hospitality. He ran to meet them, bowed before them, offered water to refresh their weary feet, and prepared a lavish feast in their honor. Abraham's hospitality went beyond mere social conventions; it reflected a profound understanding of the inherent value and dignity of every human being. His act of welcoming the strangers revealed the heart of the gospel—loving others as we have been loved by God, embracing the stranger as our own, and recognizing that by extending hospitality, we welcome the presence of God into our midst. Abraham's example is an enduring reminder that the gospel is rooted in radical hospitality, inspiring us to follow in his footsteps and extend love, kindness, and warm hospitality to all whom we encounter.

We could go on. The Mosaic law was an expression of hospitality. The cross of Jesus was an expression of hospitality. The invitation to join God in his eternal future plans is an expression of hospitality. And like all of these examples, our acts of love and kindness might also unveil the divine presence within those we receive, changing their lives forever.

Hospitality is a lifestyle of openness, welcome, and acceptance toward others, regardless of their gender, skin color, cultural background, beliefs, or behavior. It provides a sense of belonging, community, and a home to anyone who feels lost or disconnected. Hospitality is more than just inviting people over for dinner or to church, it is about truly integrating them into our lives and making them feel like insiders. Hospitality has the power to turn strangers into friends, enemies into allies, and the lost into the found.

Henri Nouwen wrote that one of the gifts that Christians bring to the world is "making our lives available to others."[8] What made Jesus' life so compelling was his availability. Jesus made everyone feel at home, even though he lacked a physical home of his own. His presence made people feel known, accepted, and loved. At every meal, whether in his own domain or as a guest of others, he was the gracious host.

In a world where cruelty and rejection abound, our simple acts of kindness and generosity wield the power to leave a lasting impact. They may serve as the sole manifestation of God's love that someone encounters in a given day or week, or even throughout their lifetime. As we practice sincere hospitality, we become vessels through which God's grace flows, lifting heavy hearts and kindling hope in the midst of the darkest circumstances.

The distinction between cultural acts of hospitality and a countercultural approach lies in our perception of others. Central to this differentiation is our understanding of whom we consider to be neighbors. Through Jesus' transformative view of hospitality, our understanding of who qualifies as a neighbor expands, challenging us to embrace a broader and more inclusive definition.

In response to the question "Who is my neighbor?" Jesus shared one of his most profound parables, featuring a Samaritan as a model of virtue.[9] As we have seen, Jesus had firsthand experience with the hospitality of Samaritans, having been welcomed into their homes and hearts for two transformative days. Forty-eight hours in the tents of those considered unclean according to the law is not something you easily forget. The love and acceptance he received there left an indelible mark on his soul, a memory that could not be easily forgotten. By sharing the parable of the good Samaritan, he not only expressed his deep appreciation for this hospitable community but also imparted a powerful lesson on the significance of demonstrating kindness and generosity to people in need.

As I reflect on Jesus' connection to the story of the good Samaritan, I can't help but wonder if this idea unfolded during his visit to Sychar. Could the parable, which has since become the universal standard for kindness and compassion, be an actual story he heard or conceived when he was a guest in that small dusty village? Such a thought invites us to consider the profound impact of this encounter on Jesus' understanding of hospitality and his teachings on loving our neighbors as ourselves. It's worth mentioning that the story of the good Samaritan is not your typical parable. We don't know whether it was the retelling of an actual event or a story that Jesus conceived to illustrate a revolutionary idea. What we do know is that it doesn't stand in isolation; it's a continuation of an idea he wants to convey about the Samaritans. He wants us to see them as worthy of love and affection. And not because they always behaved in a way that made them worthy.

The Good Samaritan

The Gospels often depict Jesus facing hard questions from religious experts, in a tradition that was commonly known as an "honor challenge." These experts would ask challenging questions to test Jesus' knowledge and expertise, with the hope of either gaining honor for themselves or shaming the rabbi.[10] But Jesus never lost an honor challenge, since he was the fulfillment of the Law and the prophets, and his answers were the personification of wisdom and authority.[11]

This encounter took place just a chapter after Jesus had prevented his disciples from calling down fire on a Samaritan village, making the question posed by the expert in the law even more poignant. He was likely expecting Jesus to judge the Samaritans for their hostility toward the Jews, but instead he was met with a response that demonstrated Jesus' mastery of the law and his deep understanding of what it truly means to love one's neighbor.

Jesus skillfully employed the Socratic teaching method by responding to the question with another question. When the expert in the law asked how to inherit eternal life, Jesus turned the inquiry back to him, asking what he believed the law required. The man correctly identified the two greatest commandments: to love God with all one's heart, soul, mind, and strength, and to love one's neighbor as oneself. Jesus affirmed his response, simply stating, "Do this and you will live."[12]

But is it truly that simple? Is the path to eternal life as straightforward as loving God wholeheartedly and loving others as we love ourselves? On the surface this may seem to be the easiest pathway to salvation, perhaps even easier than repenting of one's sins and surrendering to the work of grace, or praying the sinner's prayer, or submitting to the act of believer's baptism. But anyone who has attempted to do this for more than a day knows that it takes the power of the Holy

Spirit working in our hearts and minds to faithfully love God and neighbor.

These two commandments are the fruit of a life fully surrendered to the Spirit, not the means by which we find justification with God.

Though the concept of loving God and one's neighbor may appear deceptively simple, many of us grapple with the challenge of effectively balancing both simultaneously. It seems to be our natural inclination to prioritize one over the other. Those who prioritize loving God find fulfillment in their dedicated Bible studies, devotional time, prayer, and worship. Conversely, those who prioritize loving their neighbor draw life from acts of compassion, hospitality, and justice. We are not to choose between the two, though; we are called to embrace the beautiful tension of embodying both in our lives.

Jesus presents a transformative perspective—a third way—wherein both God and neighbor are genuinely loved and lived for. He instructs the expert to put into practice what he has proclaimed, leading to a follow-up question aimed at self-justification and proving that he already fulfills the command to love both God and neighbor. Seeking deeper understanding, the expert inquires, "Who is my neighbor?"[13]

The question at hand serves as the turning point in our understanding, becoming the crux of the matter and revealing the essential message of the parable. Jesus transcends traditional definitions, redefining the boundaries of the term *neighbor*. He doesn't simply assert, "Everyone in the whole world is your neighbor." Instead, he crafts a carefully woven parable that presents an unexpected character—a good Samaritan—as the embodiment of compassionate and caring neighborliness. This understanding invites us to reflect on our role within the narrative. Recognizing our position in the story prepares us to engage with the world in a transformative way, aligning our actions and interactions with kindness and compassion. Rich Villodas insightfully sums up the parable this way: "The Good Samaritan is a parable about being a good neighbor, compassionate spirituality, and a critique of religious passivity. And perhaps, the most important lesson stems from understanding who we are in the story."[14] It's this recognition that guides us to a more profound engagement with the world, shaping our conduct to reflect the deeper spiritual values conveyed in the story, connecting us not only with the principles of the parable but with the very essence of our faith.

In the ancient world, the term "neighbor" meant someone geographically or personally close to you. Someone in your community, in your tribe. The Greek word the legal expert uses in his question literally means "someone nearby." In the Old Testament commandment to love your neighbor as yourself that the expert was quoting, the Hebrew word means "friend" or "companion."[15]

In a culture in which another tribe could attack you at any time, people tended to draw sharp lines between those who were in their tribes and those who were not. People of other tribes were not just strangers, they were enemies. People found safety in keeping them out.

And yet, in the Old Testament, God commanded his people to treat foreigners who lived among them just as if they were native born, with all the rights and privileges of any Israelite. This law is in the same chapter as the command to love your neighbor as yourself, and it repeats that same phrase—love them (the foreigner) as yourself.[16] Yes, they fought battles against other tribes as any other nation did, but when a foreigner wanted to come live among them and join their community, they were to treat them just as they would a member of their own tribe. Like family. In God's law, from the beginning, the term "neighbor" meant both family and foreigners. It meant bringing outsiders in.

Yet by the time of Jesus, many Jewish rabbis and experts in the law had been teaching that "neighbor" meant only those of your own tribe—other Jews.[17] In the Sermon on the Mount, Jesus tells us that the rabbis of the time were teaching that you should love your neighbors (friends, family, those of your tribe), but hate your enemies. Like the Samaritans. When Jesus told them to love their enemies instead, it was radically countercultural, but he wasn't changing God's law, he was actually bringing them back to the heart of God in the Old Testament.

Loving your enemies may not change them, but it will keep them from changing you.

The religious leaders' attempt to redefine the notion of neighbor serves as a facade, masking underlying issues like ethnic resentment and religious discrimination. This kind of linguistic maneuvering is a slippery slope that we, too, can fall into when we are reluctant to step out of our comfort zones for the sake of the gospel. Such rationalizations force us to confront deeper, more uncomfortable questions about our own beliefs and motivations, including:

Do I have to love people who aren't like me? Do I have to love people who don't have the same skin color?

Do I have to love people who don't live in my zip code? Or worship my God? Or share my beliefs?

Jesus, aware of the complexity of these questions, didn't offer a simple answer. Instead, he shared this parable, which has become integral to the gospel and immortalized in the world's consciousness.

The story unfolds with four main characters: the victim traveling a perilous seventeen-mile road from Jerusalem to Jericho and the three individuals who encounter him. The treacherous road, known as "the Way of Blood," was notorious for violence, making the traveler's vicious assault, robbery, and abandonment unsurprising. What is surprising is the response of those who witnessed his plight.

The first passerby, a priest, averts his gaze and moves on toward Jericho. Jericho was a city of about twelve thousand priests, and they often traveled back and forth between their homes and the temple. We might be quick to condemn his callousness, yet his reasons might echo our own concerns. He could be wearied from temple service, or late to an important duty, or even concerned about violating laws around touching bloodied bodies.

Before long, a Levite also passes by, leaving the wounded man unattended. Once again, we're left to wonder about his motives and dare to consider how his actions mirror our own inner turmoil. Perhaps he felt overwhelmed and unqualified and even may have thought about forming a new ministry for victims of violence. Or maybe it just wasn't his thing. The "that's not my ministry" excuse is one I hear a lot as a pastor. We are all good at observing the need and suggesting new ministries, but few of us are willing to start, lead, and maintain them.

The priest's and Levite's failure was their inability to prioritize the well-being of the hurting man—the essence of the Law and the prophets. Loving God cannot be separated from attending to the hurting; indeed, loving God is intrinsically linked to aiding the suffering.[18] There is nothing in the universe that matters more to God than people who are hurting.

If you're seeking to follow God and hoping to find what he created you for, the next hurting person you encounter is likely part of the plan God has for your life.

The final passerby, a Samaritan, despised by Jews, displays empathy toward the victim. He provides first aid and ensures the man's recovery. His actions perfectly embody the concept of a good neighbor.

Jesus brilliantly positioned the characters in this parable when he identified a Samaritan as the hero. A story about a Jew helping a Samaritan would have made a powerful point as well. But portraying two pillars of the Jewish community as bad neighbors and a Samaritan as a good neighbor would have shocked his audience—just as we should be shocked when people profess their love for God but fail to see and serve their neighbors.

The expert in the law asked Jesus to define his neighbor, essentially inquiring, "Who do I 'have to' show love to?" Jesus responded not by specifying who to love but by illustrating who acted as a good neighbor. Intriguingly, the parable leaves the ethnic identity of the victim—the person we "have to" love—ambiguous. He could have been a Jew, Samaritan, Roman, Canaanite, or Ethiopian; the uncertainty implies that anyone and everyone can be our neighbor. God's love compels us to extend his love to anyone in need, regardless of distance.

Often, we think of the Great Commission as a command to go help people who are far away from us geographically, but what about reaching those far from us demographically, generationally, even ethnically?

On the eve of his assassination, Dr. Martin Luther King Jr. poured out his soul in a message on the great cost of compassion. Drawing on the parable of the good Samaritan, he challenged the conventional self-centered mentality that often guides our actions. He contrasted the concerns of the priest and the Levite, who wondered, "If I stop to help this man, what will happen to me?" with the Good Samaritan's selfless question, "If I do not stop to help this man, what will happen to him?"[19]

Dr. King's words were a powerful call to reverse our thinking, urging us to embrace a form of love that mirrors the selflessness of the Good Samaritan. He termed this selflessness "dangerous altruism," underlining that it might demand tremendous personal sacrifice, even risking our lives. The true neighbor is not hesitant to "risk his position, his prestige, and even his life for the welfare of others." This sacrifice is not in vain but a testament to every individual's inherent value and dignity. Within this context, we must grapple with the essential question of our responsibility to others, which leads us to the heart of what it means to love, serve, and be a true neighbor.

The real issue before us is: What will happen to our neighbors if we don't love them, serve them, listen to them, advocate for them, and share the gospel with them? Jesus asked the legal expert, "Which of these three do you think was a neighbor to the man who fell into the hands of robbers?" The only conceivable answer: the one who did something. Love is a verb; it is compassion in action, ministry in movement, mercy rushing to alleviate suffering.

Go and do likewise.[20]

The story of the good Samaritan was told not to build us up but to wake us up. It was designed not to comfort us but to provoke us to consider a question that is fundamental to the Christian faith: What does love require of me?

Everything.

Loving people is a messy, painful, complicated, costly activity. Those who are hurting often project their pain outward; they can be cranky, and their opinions can be sharp and cutting. People in pain have their own unique struggles and complexities. Their hurt can sometimes be transferred onto you, even unintentionally causing you harm. But that's the cross we gladly bear to extend the love of Jesus to a broken and dying generation.[21] As long as people have breath in them, we should love them without reservation.

life at longer tables

I believe the global church is at a tipping point regarding our work and our witness. After forty years of fighting the culture wars, Christians in America are more divided on social issues than ever. The walls we have built to keep us insulated from evil have proven futile, and we are left exhausted and embattled. All of this is done in the name of the one who gave his life to tear down the walls of division. Jesus calls us not to build higher walls but to build longer tables.

One of the core values at the church I serve is "we build longer tables," not only because it's the heart of Christian hospitality, but because the future of the church depends on what we will build over the next twenty years. *Will we build longer tables or higher walls?* The key to reaching our communities is not in creating better church services but in building better tables. It's not in more effective marketing but in more effective disciple-making. We need tables at which people feel welcomed, loved, valued, seen, and heard.

The church has always done its most profound work at the margins of society. Why? Because we follow a Heavenly Samaritan who exists both at the margins and in the center. Throughout the Gospels, we find Jesus at the margins. Not only did he reach out to those who existed on the margins, he experienced life there himself. Born in a small village to a poor family, a shadow of suspicion hung over his birth from the moment word of his mother's pregnancy circulated the community. From the moment he made his entrance into our world, he willingly identified with the marginalized, deliberately aligning himself with the other.[1]

The point is not to bring Jesus to the marginalized but to meet him in his chosen environment, surrounded by the people he loves. Jesus was still seen as an outsider even as his ministry grew and he gained a following of notable people. He was expelled from his hometown and continually harassed by the ecclesiastical establishment. He was ultimately mocked by the powerful, attacked by the influential, and crucified outside the walls of the city. He personified the outsider who is always on the periphery. Perhaps for this reason, the author of Hebrews exhorts us to "go to him outside the camp."[2]

Could this be why Jesus formed such a profound connection with the woman at the well? She is the epitome of the marginalized, not only in her own era but also in ours.

There is much that we don't know about the Samaritan woman's story, but one thing is clear. Their encounter is the beginning of a beautiful and enduring love affair that continues throughout his life and ministry. In his final moments, just before his glorious ascension, he entrusts his disciples with the task of spreading the gospel to the ends of the earth—geographically and demographically. And he pointedly instructs them not to overlook his cherished friends, the Samaritans.[3]

Everywhere I travel, I meet Christians who are wondering about the future of the church, faith communities, and religious institutions. How can we maintain relevance and faithfulness at a time when everything in the culture is shifting? And how can we change the world in and through coming generations? One key lies in embracing the radical love Jesus demonstrated toward the Samaritans. When our hearts are transformed by love, our actions naturally flow from a place of love. Leading with love enables us to invite others into the transformative beauty of reconciliation and redemption. Love possesses the extraordinary power to remove labels, erase scarlet letters, and dismantle divisive barriers, replacing them with longer tables of diverse people. This genuine love will redefine the church's reputation, shifting it away from one of hypocrisy and judgment and toward a new character defined by kindness and compassion.

Who are the Samaritans in your world? Who are the ones who exist at the margins and in the shadows of life?

May your love affair with them be as rich and full and rewarding as was the one Jesus enjoyed with his friends.

Yes, even those friends in the village of Sychar.

notes

Chapter 0: High Rises and Elevators

1. 2 Corinthians 5:19.
2. Luke 15:7.
3. Matthew 10:16.
4. Alan Hirsch, *The Forgotten Ways: Reactivating the Missional Church*, 5th ed. (Grand Rapids: Brazos, 2009) 78.
5. Hirsch, *Forgotten Ways*, 88.
6. Brandon T. McDaniel and Sarah M. Coyne, "'Technoference': The Interference of Technology in Couple Relationships and Implications for Women's Personal and Relational Well-Being," *Psychology of Popular Media Culture* 5, no. 1 (2016): 85–98.
7. Dr. Leonard Sweet, "Semiotics, Church and Culture," class notes, DMin lecture, George Fox University, June 18, 2021, Cannon Beach, Oregon.
8. Hari Sreenivasan, "That Time Mister Rogers Comforted Me in Real Life," PBS *NewsHour*, May 26, 2017, www.pbs.org/newshour/show/time-mister-rogers-comforted-real-life.
9. 2 Corinthians 5:19.
10. Ephesians 3:10.
11. John 20:21.
12. Dallas Willard, "A Heart-Felt Word to Pastors and Leaders," accessed August 19, 2023, https://dwillard.org/articles/heartfelt-word-to-pastors-leaders#1a.
13. John 4:4.
14. John 3:16.

Chapter 1: Unlikely Companions

1. Rich Stearns (@RichStearns), Twitter, October 22, 2022, 4:42 p.m., twitter.com/RichStearns/status/1583936933730062336.
2. John 8:48; and rabbinical literature.
3. 2 King 17:6; Daniel David Luckenbill, ed., *Ancient Records of*

Assyria and Babylonia (Chicago: University of Chicago Press, 1926; New York: Greenwood Press, 1968), 42.

4. 1 Kings 16:23–24.

5. 2 Kings 17:24.

6. Ezra 1.

7. Ezra 4:2–3.

8. Ezra 4:3–24.

9. Larry Osborne, *Accidental Pharisees: Avoiding Pride, Exclusivity, and the Other Dangers of Overzealous Faith* (Grand Rapids: Zondervan, 2012), 27.

10. Timothy Keller, *The Prodigal God: Recovering the Heart of the Christian Faith* (New York: Penguin, 2016), 18–19.

11. Sarah Pulliam Bailey, "Evangelicals Helped Get Trump into the White House. Pete Buttigieg Believes the Religious Left Will Get Him Out," *Washington Post*, March 29, 2019, www .washingtonpost.com/religion/2019/03/29/evangelicals-helped -get-trump-into-white-house-pete-buttigieg-believes-religious -left-will-get-him-out/.

12. Luke 15:1–32.

13. John 3:17.

14. John 3:1.

15. In John 19:39–40, Nicodemus brings a mixture of myrrh and aloes weighing about a hundred pounds to anoint Jesus' body for burial. The amount and type of spices used were expensive and typically associated with a burial of high honor. This has led some scholars to infer that Nicodemus was a man of means.

Chapter 2: Insiders and Outsiders

1. Tal Orian Harel, Jessica Katz Jameson, and Ifat Maoz, "The Normalization of Hatred: Identity, Affective Polarization, and Dehumanization on Facebook in the Context of Intractable

Political Conflict," *Social Media + Society* (April–June 2020): 1–10, https://doi.org/10.1177/2056305120913983.

2. 2 Corinthians 5:14.

3. In this section, I am using the terms "tribe" and "tribalism" loosely and metaphorically. I recognize that they are often used unfairly and inaccurately to simply describe a human tendency to divide into entrenched or combative factions. This is not the case for most actual historical tribal peoples. But since this usage of the word is common shorthand in our culture, I'm choosing to use it with this caveat.

4. David Brooks, *The Second Mountain: The Quest for a Moral Life* (New York: Random House, 2019), 37.

5. Patrick Miller and Keith Simon, *Truth over Tribe: Pledging Allegiance to the Lamb, Not the Donkey or the Elephant* (Colorado Springs: Cook, 2022), 188.

Chapter 3: Separation of Church and Hate

1. Genesis 12:6–7 NKJV.

2. Joshua 24:1–28.

3. Augustine, *Tractates on the Gospel of John*, 15:10.

4. Brant James Pitre, *Jesus the Bridegroom: The Greatest Love Story Ever Told* (New York: Crown, 2014), 59.

5. Genesis 21:19.

6. John 4:14.

7. Genesis 24:12–26.

8. Martin Luther King Jr., "Facing the Challenge of a New Age," address delivered at the first annual Institute on Nonviolence and Social Change, December 3, 1956, Montgomery, AL, https://kinginstitute.stanford.edu/king-papers/facing-challenge-new-age-address-delivered-first-annual-institute-nonviolence-and-social-change.

Chapter 4: Natural-Born Label Makers

1. I've heard a lot of great sermons on label making, but my favorite was by City of Grace youth pastor Adam Smith, circa 2010, which provided the inspiration for my own contribution to the idea.
2. John Vriend and Wayne W. Dyer, "Creatively Labeling Behavior in Individual and Group Counseling," *Journal of Marital and Family Therapy* 2, no. 1 (January 1976): 31–36, https://doi.org/10.1111/j.1752-0606.1976.tb00393.x.
3. Toni Morrison, *Beloved* (New York: Vintage, 2004), 225.
4. Jennifer L. Eberhardt, Nilanjana Dasgupta, and Tracy L. Banaszynski, "Believing Is Seeing: The Effects of Racial Labels and Implicit Beliefs on Face Perception," *Personality and Social Psychology Bulletin* 29 (2003): 360–70.
5. John M. Darley and Paget H. Gross, "A Hypothesis-Confirming Bias in Labeling Effects," *Journal of Personality and Social Psychology* 44 (1983): 20–33.
6. Isaiah 53:12.
7. Christine Caine, *Unashamed* (Grand Rapids: Zondervan, 2016), 70.
8. Matthew 23:23.
9. Romans 3:20–24.
10. Titus 2:11–14.
11. Brené Brown, "Want to Be Happy? Stop Trying to Be Perfect," CNN, accessed July 28, 2023, www.cnn.com/2010/LIVING/11/01/give.up.perfection/index.html.
12. Revelation 12:10.
13. Romans 8:1.
14. John 8:9–11.
15. Matthew 15:24.
16. Romans 8:1; 2 Corinthians 5:17; Ephesians 2:2–5.

Chapter 5: Truth and Tone

1. Gordon Hempton, "Silence and the Presence of Everything," May 10, 2012, in *On Being with Krista Tippett* (podcast), onbeing

.org/programs/gordon-hempton-silence-and-the-presence-of
-everything.

2. Billy Swan, "The Apostolate of the Ear," Word on Fire,
   June 9, 2022, www.wordonfire.org/articles/contributors/the
   -apostolate-of-the-ear/.

3. Dietrich Bonhoeffer, *Life Together* (London: SCM, 1954), 76.

4. Mark 5:41.

5. Tim Kreider, "Isn't It Outrageous?" *New York Times*, July 14,
   2009, archive.nytimes.com/opinionator.blogs.nytimes.com
   /2009/07/14/isnt-it-outrageous/.

6. Henri Nouwen, "Listening as Spiritual Hospitality," Henri
   Nouwen Society, March 11, 2018, henrinouwen.org/meditations
   /listening-spiritual-hospitality.

7. Hugh Whelchel, "What's Wrong with Tolerance?" Institute
   for Faith, Work and Economics, May 2, 2016, tifwe.org/whats
   -wrong-with-tolerance.

8. Dr. Mark Batterson, "Flip the Coin," sermon, National
   Community Church, Washington, DC, August 27, 2023, https://
   national.cc/media/jesus/jesus-flip-the-coin.

9. Warren W. Wiersbe, *On Being a Leader for God* (Grand Rapids:
   Baker, 2011), 39.

10. Tyler McKenzie, "Truth and Tone in an Age of Fake News,"
    Christian Standard, March 1, 2021, christianstandard.com
    /2021/03/truth-and-tone-in-an-age-of-fake-news.

11. Martin Luther King Jr., *Integrated Bus Suggestions*
    (Montgomery, AL: Montgomery Improvement Association,
    December 19, 1956), kinginstitute.stanford.edu/king-papers
    /integrated-bus-suggestions.

12. Matthew 23:37; John 2:19.

13. Tomáš Halík, *Patience with God: The Story of Zacchaeus
    Continuing in Us*, trans. Gerald Turner (New York: Doubleday,
    2009), 7.

14. Miroslav Volf, *Exclusion and Embrace: A Theological*

Exploration of Identity, Otherness, and Reconciliation, rev. ed.
(Nashville: Abingdon, 2019), 67.

15. 1 John 4:18.

16. Matthew 25:35–40.

Chapter 6: The Scarlet Letters

1. Lesbian, gay, bisexual, transgender, intersex, queer or
   questioning, asexual or aromantic, plus other sexual identities.

2. 1 Corinthians 5:1.

3. Tertullian, *On Modesty* (OrthodoxEbooks, August 10, 2018), 11.1.

4. John Chrysostom, *Commentary on Saint John the Apostle and
   Evangelist: Homilies 1–47,* Fathers of the Church 33, trans.
   Sister Goggin, Thomas Aquinas (New York: 1957), 306–9.

5. John Calvin, *The Gospel according to St. John 1–10,* trans.
   T. H. L. Parker (Grand Rapids: 1961), 90.

6. For further research, read Lynn Cohick, *Women in the World of
   the Earliest Christians* (Grand Rapids: Baker Academic, 2009).

7. Lynn Cohick, *Vindicating the Vixens: Revisiting Sexualized,
   Vilified, and Marginalized Women of the Bible* (Grand Rapids:
   Kregel Academic, 2017), 321.

8. Deuteronomy 24:1–4.

9. Divorce was "the sending away of a wife," *shilluach 'ishshah,*
   and we never read of "the sending away of a husband" in
   the Hebrew text. The feminine participle *gerushah* is a term
   applied to a divorced woman, labeling her as "the woman
   thrust out." If a wife wanted a divorce, her only recourse was to
   demand her husband divorce her.

10. Lynn H. Cohick, "Was the Samaritan Woman Really an
    Adulteress?" *Christianity Today,* October 12, 2015, www
    .christianitytoday.com/ct/2015/october/was-samaritan-woman
    -really-adulteress.html.

11. Russell Moore, "We Believe in the Power of the Gospel, Not
    the Gospel of Power," *Christianity Today,* June 7, 2023, www

.christianitytoday.com/ct/2023/june-web-only/shiny-happy
-people-duggar-gothard-russell-moore-evangelical.html.

12. Philippians 1:15–18.

13. 1 Corinthians 13:1–3.

14. Luke 7:34.

15. Mark 12:30–31.

16. Jude 1:22–23.

17. Adam Hamilton, *Half Truths: God Helps Those Who Help
Themselves and Other Things the Bible Doesn't Say* (Nashville:
Abingdon, 2016), 151.

18. Romans 2:4.

19. John 16:8.

20. Ephesians 3:17 KJV.

21. Mark 2:15.

Chapter 7: Politics, Pandemics, and Polarization

1. *As Partisan Hostility Grows, Signs of Frustration with the
Two-Party System* (Pew Research Center, August 2022), www
.pewresearch.org/politics/2022/08/09/as-partisan-hostility
-grows-signs-of-frustration-with-the-two-party-system/.

2. Russell Moore, "The State of Evangelical America," interview
by Tish Harrison Warren, *New York Times,* July 30, 2023, www
.nytimes.com/2023/07/30/opinion/state-of-evangelical-america
.html?utm_source=substack&utm_medium=email.

3. Galatians 5:22–23; Philippians 4:5; Titus 3:2; 1 Peter 3:15; James
3:17.

4. Gerald Sittser, *Resilient Faith: How the Early Christian
"Third Way" Changed the World* (Grand Rapids: Brazos, 2019).
According to Sittser, the phrase "first appeared in a second-
century letter written to a Roman official, a certain Diognetus.
The author—we don't know his name or identity—wanted to
describe the peculiar nature of Christianity to a member of the
Roman elite" (1).

5. Sittser, *Resilient Faith*, 147.

6. Psalm 23:1 KJV.

7. Galatians 1:10.

8. Matthew 5:43–45.

Chapter 8: A Tale of Two Mountains

1. Matthew Glass, "Producing Patriotic Inspiration at Mount Rushmore," *Journal of the American Academy of Religion* 62, no. 2 (Summer 1994): 265–83.

2. Joshua 8:30–35; Deuteronomy 11:26–32; 27:1–13.

3. 2 Samuel 5:7; 6:17.

4. Isaiah 2:2–4; 18:3–7; 35:8–10; 51:9–11; 60:13–14; Jeremiah 3:11–18; 31:1–9; 50:4–5; Joel 3:7–21; Obadiah 1:15–18; Micah 4:1–2; Zechariah 8:1–3.

5. Jeremiah 3:18.

6. This occurred in 722 BC. 2 Kings 17:28.

7. These events occurred in 520 BC. Ezra 4:1–5.

8. Jonathan Bourgel, "The Destruction of the Samaritan Temple by John Hyrcanus: A Reconsideration," *Journal of Biblical Literature* 135, no. 3 (Fall 2016): 505–23, https://doi.org/10.15699/jbl.1353.2016.3129.

9. John 4:23.

10. Psalm 82:3; Isaiah 1:17; Proverbs 29:7.

11. Martin Luther King Jr., "Statement on Ending the Bus Boycott," speech, December 20, 1956, Montgomery, AL, kinginstitute.stanford.edu/king-papers/documents/statement-ending-bus-boycott.

Chapter 9: The Biltmore Princess

1. Mother Teresa, *A Simple Path* (New York: Ballantine, 2007), 79.

2. Matthew 25:40.

3. Luke 4:18–19.

4. Luke 4:21.

5. Food and Agriculture Organization of the United Nations et al.,

The State of Food Security and Nutrition in the World (Rome: FAO, 2018), www.fao.org/3/I9553EN/i9553en.pdf.

6. Rasmus Hougaard and Jacqueline Carter, *Compassionate Leadership: How to Do Hard Things in a Human Way* (Boston: Harvard Business Review Press, 2022), 51–52.

7. D. Goleman, R. E. Boyatzis, and A. McKee, *Primal Leadership: Unleashing the Power of Emotional Intelligence* (Boston: Harvard Business Review Press, 2013).

8. Hougaard and Carter, *Compassionate Leadership*, 55.

9. 1 John 3:17 (KJV) *Strong's Concordance*, s.v. "G4967": "σπλάγχνον, *splánchnon, splangkh'-non*; probably strengthened from σπλήν *splēn* (the 'spleen'); an intestine (plural); figuratively, pity or sympathy:—bowels, inward affection, + tender mercy."

10. Matthew 9:6; 14:14; 15:32; 18:27; 20:34; Mark 1:41; Luke 7:13.

11. Angus Chen, "For Centuries, a Small Town Has Embraced Strangers with Mental Illness," NPR, July 1, 2016, www.npr.org /sections/health-shots/2016/07/01/484083305/for-centuries-a -small-town-has-embraced-strangers-with-mental-illness.

12. Chen, "Small Town."

13. Dave Deuel, review of *Troubled Minds: Mental Illness and the Church's Mission*, by Amy Simpson, *Themelios* 39, no. 3 (November 2014), www.thegospelcoalition.org/themelios /review/troubled-minds-mental-illness-and-the-churchs -mission.

14. World Health Organization, "The World Health Report 2001: Mental Disorders Affect One in Four People," press release, September 28, 2001, www.who.int/news/item/28-09-2001-the -world-health-report-2001-mental-disorders-affect-one-in-four -people.

15. "Anxiety Disorders," NAMI, accessed July 28, 2023, www.nami .org/About-Mental-Illness/Mental-Health-Conditions/Anxiety -Disorders.

16. Gallup, "Americans' Stress, Worry and Anger Intensified in 2018," Gallup, accessed August 17, 2023, https://news.gallup

.com/poll/249098/americans-stress-worry-anger-intensified -2018.aspx.

17. "Workplace Stress," American Institute of Stress, accessed July 28, 2023, www.stress.org/workplace-stress#.

18. Robert L. Leahy, "How Big a Problem Is Anxiety?" *Psychology Today*, April 30, 2008, www.psychologytoday.com/us/blog /anxiety-files/200804/how-big-problem-is-anxiety.

19. William H. Meller and Robert H. Albers, "Depression," in *Ministry with Persons with Mental Illness and Their Families*, ed. Robert H. Albers, William H. Meller, and Steven C. Thurber (Minneapolis: Fortress, 2019), 27.

20. Dave Deuel, review of *Ministry with Persons with Mental Illness and Their Families*, ed. Robert H. Albers, William H. Meller, and Steven D. Thurber, *Themelios* 39, no. 2 (July 2014), www.thegospelcoalition.org/themelios/review/ministry-with -persons-with-mental-illness-and-their-families.

21. 2 Corinthians 1:3–4 NKJV.

22. John 14:16; *Strong's Concordance*, s.v. "G3875": παράκλητος; an intercessor, consoler: advocate, comforter.

23. John 4:25 NKJV.

Chapter 10: Neighborhood Watch

1. Genesis 4:7.

2. Genesis 4:9.

3. Matthew 15:17–18.

4. John 4:27 NLT.

5. Luke 9:51–53.

6. Luke 9:54.

7. Luke 10:13–16.

Chapter 11: Won't You Be My Neighbor?

1. Genesis 18:1–9; 19:1–8; Judges 19:11–21.

2. Jerome H. Neyrey, *Honor and Shame in the Gospel of Matthew* (Louisville: Westminster John Knox, 1998), 190.

3. Luke 14:12–14.
4. Luke 14:23–24.
5. Acts 2:42–47.
6. Acts 4:32–35.
7. Genesis 18:1–18.
8. Henri Nouwen, "Making Our Lives Available to Others," Henri Nouwen Society, April 29, 2018, henrinouwen.org/meditations /making-lives-available-others.
9. Luke 10:25–37.
10. Luke 10:25–37.
11. Matthew 7:28; 13:54; 22:22; Mark 1:22; 11:18; 12:17; Luke 2:47; 4:22; 4:32; 20:26.
12. Luke 10:28.
13. Luke 10:29.
14. Rich Villodas, Twitter post, @richvillodas, June 7, 2020, 2:37 p.m., https://twitter.com/richvillodas/status /1269745308927483906.
15. Leviticus 19:18.
16. Leviticus 19:34.
17. Leon Morris, *The Gospel according to Matthew* (Grand Rapids: Eerdmans, 1992), 471.
18. 1 John 4:20.
19. Martin Luther King Jr., *Strength to Love* (Boston: Beacon, 2019), 26.
20. Luke 10:37.
21. John 13:35.

Epilogue

1. Isaiah 53:12.
2. Hebrews 13:13.
3. Acts 1:8.

From the Publisher

GREAT BOOKS

ARE EVEN BETTER WHEN THEY'RE SHARED!

Help other readers find this one:

- Post a review at your favorite online bookseller

- Post a picture on a social media account and share why you enjoyed it

- Send a note to a friend who would also love it—or better yet, give them a copy

Thanks for reading!